Balancing the Books

Balancing the Books

Accounting for Librarians

Rachel A. Kirk

LIBRARIES UNLIMITED

AN IMPRINT OF ABC-CLIO, LLC
Santa Barbara, California • Denver, Colorado • Oxford, England

Library of Congress Cataloging-in-Publication Data

Kirk, Rachel A.
  Balancing the books : accounting for librarians / Rachel A. Kirk.
    pages cm
  Includes bibliographical references and index.
    ISBN 978–1–61069–111–6 (pbk.) — ISBN 978–1–61069–112–3 (e-book) (print)   1. Libraries—Accounting.
2. Library finance. 3. Library finance—United States. 4. Library materials budgets—United States. I. Title.
Z683.K57   2013
025.1′1—dc23   2012031532

ISBN: 978–1–61069–111–6
EISBN: 978–1–61069–112–3

17 16 15 14 13   1 2 3 4 5

This book is also available on the World Wide Web as an eBook.
Visit www.abc-clio.com for details.

Libraries Unlimited
An Imprint of ABC-CLIO, LLC

ABC-CLIO, LLC
130 Cremona Drive, P.O. Box 1911
Santa Barbara, California 93116-1911

This book is printed on acid-free paper ∞

Manufactured in the United States of America

Contents

Foreword

Not every librarian is an accountant (or needs a full degree in accountancy), but many are responsible for making purchasing decisions, negotiating license agreements, and navigating through a maze of financial decisions. These decisions are sometimes unique to the library world—for example, licensing scholarly eBooks and eJournals or rare manuscripts that can only be obtained from a single source—and sometimes basic to any business accounting situation. Rather than librarians having to try to pick out relevant bits from an accountancy course or just learning it all on the job, librarian (and accountant) Rachel Kirk has provided them with succinct and relevant accounting basics and advice compiled in one volume.

Whether you are employed in a corporate or government library, or you work in an academic, public, or other nonprofit library, *Balancing the Books: Accounting for Librarians* has a section for you. It is both library-type specific (containing sections on differences in general accounting practices for different types of libraries) and general (covering basic accounting skills needed in any type of library).

Rachel Kirk was an accountant before she became a librarian, and she is clearly glad she made the switch to librarianship. Yet she is able to bring her accounting experience into librarianship in a way that is detailed, focused, and of immense use to librarians. The accounting information presented here is practical and applies to the day-to-day challenges facing acquisitions librarians. There is some theory ("The Philosophy of Accounting"), but this is ultimately a practical book, written by an experienced librarian to help her librarian colleagues.

Will *Balancing the Books* make you want to become an accountant, rather than or in addition to being a librarian? No, but it will help you appreciate both professions. It will also help you understand how you can become a better acquisitions or managing librarian by understanding both the practices and perspectives of accountants. Merged with your in-depth knowledge and skills of librarianship, *Balancing the Books* will provide improved confidence and improved financial management.

Carol Tenopir
Chancellor's Professor, School of Information Sciences
University of Tennessee

P.S. Rachel Kirk was my student in both her master's degree and PhD studies in library and information sciences at the University of Tennessee, but I cannot claim to have taught her any of her accountancy prowess!

Introduction

In the library and information science field, many masters of library science graduates with bachelors of arts degrees in history, English, or other liberal arts subjects find themselves responsible for multimillion-dollar budgets, licensing agreements, and procurement protocols. This phenomenon happens to graduates who become directors of public libraries, as well as librarians who manage information and research centers of corporations, law firms, and federal government agency libraries. It also happens to acquisitions librarians who operate in larger university or public library systems.

Librarians face the demands of budgets and accounting without significant preparation or mentoring in these management practices. Because librarians tend to be careful, conscientious professionals, they search for appropriate guidance and standards. However, there is a serious gap in existing literature regarding accounting principles for libraries, particularly in the area of acquisitions accounting—this gap prevents librarians from acquiring the necessary knowledge base. Established librarians are frustrated by the responsibility and the current pace of changes, and new acquisitions librarians are bewildered.

The idea for this book originated in a presentation I gave at the November 2009 Charleston Conference. I was concerned that there would be little interest in the topic of accounting basics for librarians. To my surprise, the room was packed with interested and engaged librarians. Near the end of the session, several librarians stated that this session was as much training in acquisitions or budgeting as they had ever received. Many librarians even stayed afterward to ask questions. Since then I have been invited to other libraries to work with acquisitions staff, and I have been asked to give presentations and workshops at state and national conferences.

These responses and invitations suggest that librarians are at a tipping point to demand instruction in accounting and acquisitions that will prepare them for their responsibilities. This book provides an overview of accounting and budgeting techniques that apply to most libraries.

Two major components of financial management exist in library accounting: material expenditures and general operating expenditures. This book focuses on the materials budget first because of its specialized budgeting and accounting issues, whereas issues associated with operating expenditures share many similarities with other organizations in the same category (federal agency libraries, corporate or law libraries, public libraries, and academic libraries). Library directors and managers deal with operating expenditures in addition to those related to acquiring library materials. General operating expenditures include all costs associated with the operation of the library: employee salaries, including benefits and continuing training; rent; utilities; supplies; insurance; and other costs associated with running an organization.

In some libraries, the director or manager also handles the materials budget. In larger libraries, an acquisitions librarian takes over this responsibility. The materials budget includes expenditures for books, periodicals, databases, video games, maps, and other materials that comprise the collection of the library.

This book does not address payroll accounting. Payroll accounting includes salary and wage expenses and generally comprises 50–70% of a library's budget. So payroll accounting is quite important to a library's financial management. However, proprietary systems to manage payroll accounting are implemented in most libraries, so although library directors do manage salary and wage accounting and budget issues, the parent organization or government unit usually specifies procedures. Sometimes the parent organization provides additional guidance and technology to address these costs.

Moving on from the experiences of librarians, the second section of this book explains accounting and regulatory requirements of different types of libraries. This section explains the differences between federal, government, and private nonprofit and for-profit libraries; introduces the government agency that guides the reporting requirements for the different library types; and provides exemplary financial statements for each category. Government and private nonprofit libraries receive the most attention because they represent the largest proportion of libraries in the United States.

The second section also explains the basic accounting activities of classifying, recording, summarizing, and reporting, as well as how these daily functions support accounting records such as the general ledger and, ultimately, the financial statements. The chart of accounts will be discussed as the classification schema for accounting activities. This portion of the book also focuses on the importance of funds and their function in the library financial structure.

In addition to these overall accounting concepts, the second section returns to acquisitions accounting to explain how to create a subsidiary ledger. Using the acquisitions module of the integrated library system (ILS), one can create a subledger to track library materials by reporting objectively while simultaneously supporting the materials balance in the general ledger.

The section closes by introducing the topic of internal controls and how they guard the library's assets. One chapter in this section concentrates on the importance of reconciliations, providing an overview, flowcharts, and examples of reconciliations.

The third section, budgeting, begins with a philosophical view of budgeting and develops into specific techniques for creating and monitoring the budget. In addition, this section provides examples of how to use budget information to control future costs through analysis and negotiation.

Existing State of Accounting in the Library Science Field

This section addresses the experience of acquisitions librarians (Chapter 1) and library directors responsible for financial management (Chapter 2). Chapter 3 explores the preparation provided for both positions by American Library Association-accredited masters programs. Chapter 4 discusses skill sets necessary for resource management as an acquisitions librarian or a library director.

Job Responsibilities of Acquisitions Librarians

If you feel unprepared, you are not alone. Most directors or managers of public libraries, as well as acquisitions librarians, are surprised by the amount of accounting necessary to their positions. Their plight has been exacerbated by the recent budget situation, in which they now need to project future financial needs as well as analyze the cost effectiveness of long-standing products and purchasing practices.

Librarians have asked most frequently about what factors to consider in creating budgets, how to create useful fund ledgers, and how to reconcile between fund ledgers and the general ledger accounts of the parent institution. Other questions include how to account for hosting and access fees and how to quickly identify resources for cuts if a budget situation turns dire.

Changing Environment of Library Acquisitions

Once upon a time, librarians bought books. Librarians bought journals. Librarians paid for what they would own until the pages disintegrated or the title was lost, stolen, or destroyed. It was not necessarily an easier time. Challenges existed. Integrated library systems were considerably less sophisticated than they are today. Librarians recorded orders and payments for monographs and subscriptions on spreadsheets, sometimes on paper ledgers. The work was tedious and error prone.

The last few months of the fiscal year often forced additional challenges on acquisitions librarians and staff. Money left over in a government entity's general fund often found its way back to the library materials fund, because that was one of the few ways that an institution could spend money that did not create a future obligation (liability) of financial resources. Acquisitions departments often found themselves with an extra 25% of the budget to expend *and* account for in the last two months of the year. This situation created a flurry of spending activity and difficult circumstances for accounting.

Approval plans helped public and academic libraries regulate spending levels more evenly throughout the fiscal year and eased accounting by channeling invoicing through one (or more) major vendor. Additionally, it became increasingly popular for libraries to partner with one or more major vendors ("jobbers") to streamline their purchasing of books and outsource the cataloging and processing so that the books would arrive at the library "shelf-ready."

For acquisitions librarians charged with the responsibility of periodicals, vendors such as Ebsco, Harrassowitz, and Swets provided a centralized subscription management service. These subscription management services allowed libraries to outsource much of the acquisitions process for most of their titles for a service fee. The fee was computed as a percentage of each title's list price and adjusted by volume discounts for business conducted between that library and the subscription agent.

Unfortunately, subscription agents have never been able to filter all periodical acquisitions work because some smaller or specialized presses do not contract with them. Although the percentage of these titles has been relatively low for most libraries for many years, these titles create a disproportionate amount of work for acquisitions librarians and staff. As a result, the business processes of smaller presses sometimes do not reflect mainstream periodical acquisitions practices. This situation leaves the acquisitions librarian and staff with the responsibility of finding ways to adapt to idiosyncratic contracts, licenses, invoicing, and payment expectations.

The most recent changes in acquisitions have occurred with the increasing popularity of books, journals, and even data sets in electronic format. The availability of these formats and increases in technological platforms have opened up options for firm ordering and subscription ordering for all of these formats. In addition, these materials may be acquired through consortia arrangements within a group of participating libraries. Accounting and budgeting for materials acquired through consortia adds yet another layer of complexity to the acquisitions process.

During the Acquisitions Institute at Timberline Lodge held in May 2000, participant groups unanimously listed Budgeting/Financial Management, Management Skills/Supervision, and Knowledge of the Publishing Industry/Book Trade as the most important core competencies held by acquisitions librarians (Fisher 2001, 185). Fisher concluded that an acquisitions librarian must "have some knowledge of fiscal management and automated library systems" (ibid.).

In the last 10 years, acquisitions librarianship has continued to become more complex, with more diverse and costly materials. Acquisitions librarians' responsibilities currently include acquiring books, serials, and individual license media directly through publishers like Scholastic or through wholesalers like Baker and Taylor, Midwest, Ambassador, and Ingram. Acquisitions librarians also create, monitor, and weed standing orders and monograph serial continuations, as well as subscribe to journals through subscription agents such as Ebsco or directly with the publisher. Acquisitions librarians create, tailor, or at least monitor approval plans; select individual works that support the collection; and communicate with faculty, graduate students, and other librarians about works acquired.

In addition, the acquisitions librarian also works with publishers and aggregators to license databases, electronic journals, and electronic books, which can be purchased individually like print books. Acquisitions librarians act as the primary negotiator on these procurements and are responsible for shepherding the license and/or contract through the parent organization. Acquisitions librarians work with librarians from other institutions to create consortia that can share the cost and access of collections of electronic resources. Typically, the acquisitions librarian must follow the provisions of the umbrella consortia contract as well as a separate contract for his or her library.

Library materials can be acquired in many different ways these days. Patron-driven acquisition is the most recent form of procurement for electronic books. In patron-driven acquisitions programs, a preselected population of books is loaded into the catalog, and to the patron, these records look identical to other catalog records. (The records indicate the book's electronic format so the patron knows to expect that.) When the patron selects the record, the electronic book automatically downloads for them. After a predetermined trigger point passes, that electronic book is considered "sold" to the library and becomes a permanent part of the collection. On a regular basis, the vendor communicates to the library which books have been acquired through this process and invoices the library for these works. Electronic book collections can also be acquired through subscriptions, whereby the library pays a subscription fee for access to a collection of electronic books for a period of time, usually one year.

Acquisitions librarians must create the workflows for these diverse procurement channels. These workflows begin with a request for a resource, graduating to an order, receipt, and payment for the work, as well as documentation of vendor and price information. They typically culminate with the transfer of the work to the cataloging department for successful integration into the current catalog.

Most acquisitions departments depend on the work of library assistants who specialize in specific areas such as paying vendor invoices, managing continuations, or concentrating on specific vendors. Acquisitions librarians supervise the work of these employees. Typically, the librarian designs and implements training on new vendor systems and integrated library systems, tests workflows for efficiency, and redesigns these workflows to meet changing processes. The librarian works with the supervised employees to troubleshoot workflow issues and resolve problems. Frequently in acquisitions work, predetermined workflows do not meet the needs of acquiring a specific object. Therefore, the librarian and the acquisitions staff communicate regularly to solve problems for special cases. Acquisitions librarians already know that there are often just as many special cases as there are "normal" ones.

Fiscal management is another duty of acquisitions librarians. They must document the accounting activity of acquisitions, monitor acquisitions spending against the budget, and verify the recording of acquisitions transactions in both the parent organization's accounting system and the library acquisitions module.

In addition to handling the accounting for acquisitions expenditures, the acquisitions librarian is often asked to create budget forecasts for future years. Knowing current spending patterns helps the acquisitions librarian create reasonable estimates for future budget cycles.

Other situations that require the acquisitions librarian's attention include those which require expertise about specific processes—for example, when grants or gifts have been obtained for the acquisition of books or other library materials. The acquisitions librarian must make sure that these expenditures are tracked separately and also maintain the appropriate documentation for reimbursement from the grant. Another example occurs where the acquisitions librarian collaborates with professionals from various areas within the library as well as external stakeholders. For instance, the acquisitions librarian works with circulation to determine the best course of action for lost or missing books, and he or she contributes to assessment of library programs by providing information on those programs' expenditures.

What Current Advertisements in ALA JobList Tell Us about Acquisitions Librarian Positions

It is worth noting that acquisitions librarian job descriptions include more detail than descriptions for director positions. A search of the American Library Association (ALA) JobList yielded 21 results for a keyword search of "acquisitions" performed on January 2, 2012. These results represent a snapshot in time.

Of the 21 acquisitions librarian positions listed, 16 were at academic libraries, 3 were at public libraries, 1 was at a special library, and 1 was a duplicate. Six of the descriptions included budgeting as a job responsibility (29%). Other than budgeting, the most popular or frequently listed job responsibilities for acquisitions librarians included supervising staff (50%); collaborating with other departments (41%); handling electronic resources and licenses (41%); designing, monitoring, and modifying workflows to increase efficiency (32%); troubleshooting user access problems or invoice issues (32%); applying new technologies (32%); developing and/or managing collections (27%); and, finally, collection assessment (23%).

These job advertisements did not include the terms "accounting" or "financial management," although some included phrasing about budgeting or resolving invoice issues, as reflected above. Professionals in financial services would think it odd that budgeting be considered a stand-alone skill. The ability to budget depends on an understanding of accounting and finance and how those disciplines measure economic and operational activity. Attempting to budget without having a foundation in accounting and financial management is analogous to making determinations without prior evidence, assumptions, or logic. How do you reach conclusions? What is the methodology?

Resolving invoice issues requires some basic accounting skills, such as extending prices per units of quantity and tracking requests, purchase orders, invoices, and payments through a purchasing and/or accounting system. Designing, monitoring, and modifying workflows necessitates an understanding of how receiving requests transitions to other steps in the process—creating purchase orders with a book vendor, tracking those orders internally through an acquisitions system, receiving the books, ensuring proper payment, and classifying the amounts paid for the books in the organization's ledger. So despite its lack of mention in most of the job advertisements for librarian positions that deal with money, budgeting, and planning, accounting serves as a foundation for all the other skills necessary for sound financial management.

Assessing the Accounting and Financial Composition of Acquisitions Librarianship

Some library directors reluctantly acknowledge the complexities involved with the financial and accounting responsibilities of acquisitions librarians. Perspectives may have evolved this way because the position exists within a field that, historically, has not embraced financial or quantitative skill sets. Because of institutional discomfort with tracking money, acquisitions librarians focused on selection and collection development responsibilities and avoided financial, accounting, and budgeting issues. Accounting and budgeting issues arose with specific problems, such as negative audit findings (accounting) or layoffs (budget cuts). Accounting and budgeting earned a negative reputation within the library, and from without, libraries and library employees were unkindly labeled "cost" centers—rather than being considered skill and resource investments put into the collective intellectual treasury of the organization.

Description of Purchasing Agent in Government Agency as a Model for Acquisitions

Reframing accounting and financial management skills within the context of acquisitions allows librarians to acquire the education they need to understand the multiple facets of their jobs in a more generalized context of complex twenty-first-century organizations. Education prepares these professionals to expect, adapt to, and transform both the marketplace that they participate in as agents representing the needs of their institutions and their internal environments. Comparing the responsibilities of acquisitions librarians to those of purchasing or procurement managers in other industry sectors reveals similarities in financial and accounting functions.

What would best serve us is a model of a nonprofit or government position that specializes in acquisitions, outside of a library or information center environment—this type of model would illustrate the essential functions, divorced from our ordinary schema. Such a position exists in the form of a purchasing agent for a government agency. This position parallels an acquisitions librarian in the nonlibrary world in several ways. Like acquisitions librarians, these professionals procure the best and most relevant resources at the lowest possible cost. They must have a working technical knowledge of the resources needed and stay aware of changes in the industry by attending conferences and trade shows. In making decisions, they consider price, quality, availability, reliability, as well as the quality of technical support provided by the service or product (U.S. Bureau of Labor Statistics 2011). In addition, purchasing agents analyze the performance of their vendors.

Purchasing agents, like acquisitions librarians, strive to respond quickly to the changing needs of their patrons. Like librarians working with collection development teams, purchasing agents work collaboratively with a variety of experts to identify strengths and weaknesses of resources prior to purchase. The following example illustrates how this collaboration takes place:

> Purchasing professionals often work closely with other employees in a process called "team buying." For example, before submitting an order, the team may discuss the design of custom-made products with company design engineers, the problems involving the quality of purchased goods with production supervisors, or the issues in shipping with managers in the receiving department. This additional interaction improves the quality of buying by adding different perspectives to the process. (ibid.)

Skills expected of purchasing agents include an understanding of material requirements and inventory systems, researching of suppliers and markets, proficiency with various software packages, the ability to analyze technical data, good communication skills, negotiation abilities, mathematical aptitude, and the ability to perform financial analyses (ibid.).

Education requirements for purchasing agents include a bachelor's degree. Many employers prefer coursework or even a master's degree in economics, finance, accounting, applied science, or engineering. Advancement to a senior purchasing manager position typically requires a master's degree (ibid.).

Chapter 2

Fiscal Management Responsibilities of Library Directors

Budgets of public libraries average $1,186,578. (This number is calculated by dividing total operating expenditures of $10,946,186,000 by the number of libraries [9,225], as reported by the Institute of Museum and Library Services [IMLS] 2011, 124.) In comparison, the budgets of most academic libraries are higher, at around $1,851,209. (This amount is calculated by dividing total operating expenditures of $6,829,108,368 by the number of libraries [3,689], as reported by National Center for Education Statistics [NCES] 2011, 12.) With average financial responsibility ranging from $1.1 million to $1.8 million, library directors need preparation in accounting concepts, regulation and reporting requirements, and budgeting techniques.

Library directors face financial pressures beyond the material budgets. In 1999, personnel expenditures of public libraries represented 64% of operating expenditures (NCES 2002, 72). By 2009, these same expenditures had crept upward to 66.6% (IMLS 2011, 121).[1] Health insurance premium increases have affected public libraries like all other businesses. On average, staffing increased from 12.2 to 15.6 full-time equivalent employees per library.

For academic libraries, salary and wages held steady at 50% of expenditures, but average full-time equivalent staff decreased from 27 to 24 from 2000 to 2010 (NCES 2003, 35; NCES 2011, 12).

The levels of complexity faced by financial decision makers in the library (acquisitions librarians or library directors) continues to increase simultaneously with escalating budget pressures, demands for fiscal accountability, and declining federal and state funding sources. In some systems, the director shoulders the financial responsibility of the library. Increasingly, however, assistant directors share more of these responsibilities as directors face increasing demands for fundraising activities. This relatively new shift in increasing financial sophistication may take aspiring library directors and assistant directors by surprise.

> For example, it is the assistant director's responsibility to implement the budgets, monitor expenditures, provide tracking reports, and keep departments on their monetary targets. These budgetary duties are similar to those of the acquisitions librarian, although on a larger scale. (Barstow 2002)

How Library Director Jobs Are Described in ALA JobList

The ALA JobList[2] was searched to explore how director positions are described to job seekers and other members of the library and information science audience. In a key word search of "director" that left all other search terms open, 73 job advertisements were retrieved from those posted between November 1, 2011 and January 1, 2012. These results represent a snapshot in time. Of these 73 results, 3 were duplicates of earlier descriptions that had been revised and reposted, 50 advertisements represented actual director positions, and the remainder included the word "director" in the description.[3]

Even among the 70 results that retrieved library director positions, 19 of the 70 positions described specialized director positions reaching beyond the traditional roles of librarians. Examples of these positions included "director of heritage resources"; "director of development"; "teaching and learning services coordinator"; "director of emerging technologies and community services"; "director of community services"; "executive director, global member engagement and metadata services"; and "director, human resources and diversity programs." These descriptions are included because they provide useful examples of how librarianship articulates needs for successful transition in the twenty-first century beyond the traditional understanding of librarian leadership. Librarianship also needs to extend and develop its requirements for accounting and financial management.

Out of the 50 advertisements for director positions, 16 of them were at public libraries, 29 were at academic libraries, and 5 were at libraries categorized as "other." Within this population of 50 advertisements, 25 (50%) directly referenced the need for budgeting experience, with 10 (20%) of these advertisements provided the annual budget. Of the 25 positions, 4 stated financial management as a responsibility and 1 mentioned fiscal responsibility. Twenty-three positions listed the need for strategic planning. Twelve positions required the director to assess activities against outcomes. Eleven advertisements listed the ability to secure external funding. Only 8 advertisements listed accounting (2) or reporting (6) requirements, which is surprising because accounting and reporting skills provide the foundation for assessment, budgeting, financial management, and strategic planning. One job listing for a public library specified that the director needed bookkeeping skills.

In general, the library profession seems to lack understanding of how detail-oriented skills such as accounting, recording, and compiling financial data connect with the extremely important leadership functions of reporting, budgeting, and assessing activity. This gap is ironic in an information discipline that captures and describes individual items and integrates them into classification schema. The fundamental logic of connections between broader and narrower categories of concepts already exists within librarians. The missing link appears to be how financial data connects together.

Another observation is that several of these advertisements stated that the applicant should have solid budget and/or financial management expertise. The implication is that these skills would be already developed prior to taking this position, but where does the training ground for these skills exist? Certainly not in the associate directorships in reference and instruction services which were included in the results for directors. These positions generally had no budget or financial responsibility.

Investments

Especially problematic is a library director's responsibility to manage or monitor investments on behalf of a public library or nonprofit library. In a public library, the library board should have at least one fiscal officer that guides investment activities and a sound investment policy. In a nonprofit library, the library director probably communicates with trustees or board members who have responsibility for endowment and investment accounts, but the director does not actively manage these accounts. In private corporate or otherwise profit-oriented private sector libraries, investment is probably handled separately from the library. However, library directors of public libraries remain responsible for all of the library's activities and need to understand the nature of investments and cost-benefit analysis.

Library directors, specifically those at public libraries and nonprofit libraries, need to have a basic understanding of investments, as they are sometimes expected to invest available budgeted operating funds until necessary and monitor endowment funds for special purposes. Larger public libraries often have foundations as legally separate tax-exempt components of the library. These foundations serve to raise and hold funds in support of the library and its programs. While the director's relationship with the foundation and its separate board of directors may vary, library directors need a basic understanding of investments, rates of return, and purchasing power.

The basis of this understanding begins with the time value of money, an intuitive economic concept that a dollar today is preferable to a dollar to be received in the future. Money has time value because of the opportunity that exists to loan or borrow at an additional amount (interest) that is compounded over time, as well as its relationship to inflation and decreased purchasing power over a specific time period. The time value of money includes the calculations of present value and future value. The interest rates in these calculations provide a baseline for comparing investment returns, since investing extra capital (equities) represents an opportunity cost to loaning extra capital (in the debt market—such as corporate or municipal bonds). The concept of a return on investment forms the basis of other cost-benefit analysis that should be performed in purchasing decisions, such as deciding between alternative financial commitments—for example, to rent or lease property for public use, to rent or buy places for off-site materials storage, or to buy or lease computers.

Library Investments

In some libraries, investments represent a major, if not the major, source of revenue. The library manages these investments by appointing a special board, sometimes referred to as an investment committee. The investment committee appoints managers or manages the funds themselves. Generally, these members serve without compensation and are indemnified (held harmless) against actions that they have taken in good faith even if the investments lose value.

Investment committees often appoint managers or manage endowment funds. Endowment funds are excess cash held in applicable accounts is invested for certain periods of time. Generally, the investment earnings from that account can be withdrawn and spent on the library, but the original amount must never be spent. Only the interest received from these investments can be used to fund the library. Library directors and library boards attempt to maximize the earnings from these funds while protecting the underlying principal. Typically the board will create and vote on an investment policy.

The goal of an investment policy is to provide clear objectives and limitations to the investment committee. These objectives and limitations aid them in their goal of achieving a real rate of return without decreasing the purchasing power of the fund's principal after distributions to the library. In private nonprofit libraries with investment committees, the board of directors generally meets annually to determine the amount of money to be drawn from an endowment fund for the following fiscal year. The amount of money withdrawn will be based on an average investment performance of the fund over the preceding three years. In some cases, the investment policy specifies minimum and maximum distribution amounts, such as a range between 2.0% and 5.0% of the average size of the fund during the measurement period.

The library foundation board provides clear direction to the investment committee regarding what investments are considered financially sound enough to warrant inclusion in the library's portfolio. An example from the Princeton Public Library Foundation (2008, 2) states,

Asset Mix: Assets can be distributed among equities, fixed income and convertible securities, index tracking instruments (e.g., "spiders"), Federal Instrumentalities, mutual funds, and other funds registered with the SEC. The Investment Committee will determine the tactical weighting of asset classes of the portfolio within the following target ranges:

	High	Low
Equity/Equity Funds	75%	50%
Fixed Income/Fixed Income Funds	50%	25%
Cash Equivalents	20%	0%

The Westchester Public Library of Westchester, Indiana, provides a good example of an investment policy, *Westchester Public Library Investment Policy* (2011), in which the director of the public library is designated as the investing officer. The policy states that its purpose is to provide maximum security and achieve highest investment returns while meeting daily cash flow needs, in compliance with Indiana code 5-13-9.

The *Westchester Public Library Investment Policy* also states its objectives in terms of safety, liquidity, and return on investment. The scope of the library's investment activity is limited to Indiana code 5-13-9, which includes "any security backed by the full faith and credit of the United States Treasury or fully guaranteed by the United States; and issued by the United States Treasury, a federal agency, or a federal instrumentality, or a federal government sponsored enterprise" (Westchester Public Library 2011, 1–2). The library director's responsibility to the finance board at Westchester includes maintaining documentation that supports quotes of the specific rates of interest for the term of the investment, as well as placing the investment with the designated depository quoting the highest rate of interest (or else selecting between two or more depositories tied at the highest quote). The library director must obtain and document quotes to receive bids for the library's invested funds and negotiate the sale of investments for the purpose of depositing the proceeds into the library's checking account. Each year at the first meeting of the board of directors, the library director must provide a written report to the financial board concerning the investment of Westchester Public Library funds for the prior fiscal year (Westchester Public Library 2011, 1–2).

Description of a Financial Manager as a Model for Financial Responsibilities of a Library Director

As discussed in Chapter 1, job postings for acquisitions librarian and library director positions need to be reframed to emphasize the necessary accounting and financial management skills.

While comparing acquisitions librarians to purchasing agents in federal or state government substantiated the responsibilities of the acquisitions librarians, comparing library directors to industry counterparts proves more difficult. The closest comparison that represents the financial responsibilities of a library director (while clearly not addressing the types of programs managed or social responsibilities inherent in the position) was the position description of financial managers from the *Occupational Outlook Handbook*. The subgroups of financial managers who shared responsibilities with library directors are listed below:

- Financial managers oversee the preparation of financial reports, direct investment activities, and implement cash management strategies. Managers also develop strategies and implement the long-term goals of their organization. . . .

- Treasurers and finance officers direct their organization's budgets to meet its financial goals. They oversee the investment of funds, manage associated risks, supervise cash management activities, and execute capital-raising strategies to support the firm's expansion.

- Cash managers monitor and control the flow of cash receipts and disbursements to meet the business and investment needs of their firm. For example, cash flow projections are needed to determine whether loans must be obtained to meet cash requirements or whether surplus cash can be invested. . . .

- Branch managers of financial institutions administer and manage all of the functions of a branch office. Job duties may include hiring personnel, approving loans and lines of credit, establishing a rapport with the community to attract business, and assisting customers with account problems. Branch managers also are becoming more oriented toward sales and marketing. As a result, it is important that they have substantial knowledge about the types of products that the bank sells. Financial managers who work for financial institutions must keep abreast of the rapidly growing array of financial services and products. For example, government financial managers must be experts on the government appropriations and budgeting processes. (U.S. Bureau of Labor Statistics, 2011)

Although the analogy between library director and financial manager is not obvious, the library director is also responsible for overseeing the preparation of financial reports, directing investment activities, and implementing cash management strategies, as well as developing strategies and implementing the long-term goals of goals of the library, as described in the first bullet point of the excerpt. The following paragraphs take the language used of financial managers and modify the descriptions to apply to library contexts.

The treasury function discussed in the excerpt's second bullet point also fits. A library director sets up his or her organization's budget to meet its financial goals, oversees the investment of funds, manages associated risks, supervises cash management activities, and executes capital-raising strategies to support the firm's expansion. A capital-raising strategy might include a grant program or a construction project funded by a municipal bond.

Library directors act as cash managers (as discussed in the third bullet point) by monitoring and controlling the flow of cash receipts and disbursements to meet the business needs of their firm. For example, cash flow projections are needed to determine whether loans must be obtained to meet cash requirements or whether surplus cash can be invested in accordance with the library's investment policy.

The last bullet point discussed a branch manager of a financial institution. This last description represents the most compelling and challenging vision of a library director because of the breadth of the responsibilities included in the article, but most importantly, because of the depth of relationships the library director must cultivate with the community and its members. Internally, job duties entail hiring personnel, approving decisions and purchases, assisting with library patrons, and performing the other financial responsibilities explored in the cash and treasury management functions. Externally, library directors must establish a rapport with the community to attract individual patrons and businesses, become more oriented toward marketing the strengths of the library to the specific needs of the community, and, accordingly, possess a deep knowledge of their collection and the individual and collective talents of their employees. Library directors must always keep abreast of the rapidly growing array of technology and information products and services so that their libraries are able to assimilate the best practices of other sectors. In addition, a director of a municipal or state library must be highly knowledgeable about government appropriations and budgeting processes.

Given the financial responsibilities described above, librarians aspiring to be library directors should actively develop broad skill sets by taking courses offered in library and information science programs as well as courses offered in colleges of business or public administration. Taking advantage of internship possibilities in nontraditional settings (for library students) such as banks and in traditional library settings working directly under a library director can provide for an expanded perspective of the skills and abilities necessary.

Notes

1. According to the Library of Congress, personnel wages and benefits comprised 50% of the budget for 2010 (Library of Congress 2011, 38).

2. The ALA JobList site has advanced search options that include fields for keyword searching (multiple keywords are separated by commas); city; state(s); library type(s); job category(ies); position type(s); minimum salary, years of experience, degree(s) required, and institution(s) (ALA at http://joblist.ala.org/modules/jobseeker/advancedsearch.cfm).The "job category(ies)" and "position type(s)" options approximated my interest in directorship, but instead of using their search terms ("administrative/management" in the case of "job category(ies)" and "full-time" in the case of "position type(s)"), I used the keyword "director." The term "director" increased both relevancy and retrieval for the types of responsibilities I sought.

3. No option existed to search only by job title. The other 22 positions either reported to the director or a board of directors but did not include the usual responsibilities associated with directorships. These positions included "library children's services manager," "director of collection management," "library branch manager," "head of library systems," "geosciences and maps librarian," "public services librarian/liaison to the school of education and human development," "preservation librarian," "art and architecture librarian," "metadata analyst," "library digital infrastructure and technology coordinator," "systems librarian I/II/III," "community services manager," and "university archivist," among others.

Chapter 3

Acquisitions or Accounting Preparation in Library and Information Science Programs

If you are a library and information science (LIS) student interested in becoming an acquisitions librarian, you should take a class in technical services. The technical services class may or may not include a section on acquisitions. Take the class anyway, because the knowledge that you acquire about how technical services departments work, as well as the instruction in cataloging principles, will serve you well in an acquisitions environment. Consider taking a class in advanced database searching as well, as it will expose you to many of the different databases and their vendors. Many times the vendors send representatives to these classes to provide training and to talk about their products and companies.

At a minimum, you should certainly take the management class that addresses budgeting and fiscal management. If your program allows you to take a practicum or obtain field experience, arrange for one that includes an acquisitions component. You will need to identify an acquisitions librarian who is willing to be your practicum supervisor early in the semester prior to the one in which you plan to take the practicum.

There are currently 63 ALA-accredited LIS programs. A review of their recent course listings identified courses that mentioned acquisitions or budgeting in the title. The course descriptions for technical services often listed acquisitions. However, acquisitions appeared among other broad topics such as cataloging and preservation, so it was difficult to determine from the course descriptions alone how in depth the courses treated acquisitions topics.

If you can identify which courses in your program offer exposure to acquisitions topics, take them to see how much you enjoy the classes. If you find you enjoy these classes as much or more than other classes in the curriculum, augment your coursework with some more accounting and/or finance/budgeting classes.

Almost all of the 63 ALA-accredited programs offer at least one course in library management. The library management courses' descriptions usually included the word "budgeting." Again, keep in mind that many leadership and management topics are included in these courses, and it is impossible to see how deeply the topic of budgeting is explored. However, the limited amount of LIS literature devoted to material budgeting for libraries suggests that budgeting is not extensively taught. The inclusion of budgeting into leadership and management courses suggests that budget management is considered a skill necessary only for higher-level managers or library directors. Students interested in acquisitions may not realize that the leadership class may be one of the curriculum's few introductions to budgeting.

The course titles and descriptions within the 63 ALA-accredited masters programs showed several patterns regarding acquisitions topics and where in the curriculum that they are taught.

Acquisitions topics are introduced in courses or course series named "Technical Services" or under a course, often part of the core curriculum, named "Collection Management" or "Managing Library Collections," as in the case of the University of Wisconsin–Milwaukee (University of Wisconsin–Milwaukee 2012).

According to its course description, "520: Managing Library Collections" covers

> theory and practice of collection management across formats including *selection* tools and criteria, *acquisition* and *evaluation* of collections, deselection, preservation, and other *collection development* topics. (ibid., emphasis added)

A few programs, such as the one at the University of South Carolina, offer an advanced elective course. The course offered in this program, "766: Collection Development and Acquisitions," requires three prerequisites (University of South Carolina 2012). These prerequisite courses ("Introduction to Technical Services," "Introduction to Information Sources and Services," and "Introduction to the Management of Libraries, Media Centers, and Information Agencies") provide students with an overview of the LIS field.

Many programs offer an advanced elective course in management that covers financial and personnel management. Not all course descriptions provide enough information to estimate the depth of detail in which financial topics will be covered. However, basic coverage of budgeting principles is a reasonable assumption for financial management courses. These courses may be listed with such titles as "Management; Management of Libraries and Information Services" (University of Wisconsin–Milwaukee 2012); "Financial and Human Resource Management in Information Agencies" at University of North Texas (http://www.lis.unt.edu/main/ViewPage.php?cid=36); "Management Theory and Practice for Information Professionals" at University of California, Los Angeles (http://is.gseis.ucla.edu/academics/degrees/mlis/); "Planning, Evaluation, and Financial Management" at Florida State University (http://online.fsu.edu/courseofferings/coursearchive/grad/infoStudies.cfm); and "Management of Information Programs and Services" (Dearstyne 2010). The University of Illinois at Urbana–Champaign offers "Financial Management" (http://www.lis.illinois.edu/), which emphasizes obtaining financial support from grants and contracts. The University of Denver offers an entire course, "Grantwriting and Fundraising," on these topics (http://www.du.edu/education/programs/lis/descriptions.html).

Despite the dispersion of acquisitions and budgeting topics into various LIS courses, future library directors or managers and acquisitions librarians do not receive prolonged and intensive education in these areas. Even if both acquisitions and budgeting topics are offered to students through the different courses, the students may not see the connection or take all of the various courses needed to get the necessary breadth of perspective. The budgeting section of a management class may not relate to the budgeting issues faced by acquisitions. The detailed transaction accounting used in acquisitions is unlikely to be addressed in the management course. In addition, these courses draw students who are interested, at least initially, in different career paths or curricular concentrations (technical services versus management, academic versus public).

Management, leadership, and technical service courses are not the only places that offer acquisitions preparation. Taking courses in systems design and analysis will provide skills that allow one to conceptualize an integrated library system (ILS), an acquisitions module, an electronic resources management system, and the institution's enterprise resource management system (such as Banner, PeopleSoft, or SAP). Clarion University (http://www.clarion.edu/25473/) offers an "Information Management Systems" course that specifically includes acquisitions systems as part of its focus. University of Maryland offers a "Library Systems Analysis" course that focuses on managerial decision making and problem solving, modeling systems, flowcharting, performing cost analyses, designing systems, and evaluating through various methods (http://ischool.umd.edu/content/LBSC-Course-Descriptions#c603).

Beyond Coursework

During your early career, try to work with and learn from as many librarians as possible. As soon as you acquire the fundamental skills to perform your job, volunteer for duties outside of your assigned responsibility to broaden your perspective and get to know your colleagues. If you begin your career in systems or technical services, volunteer to work a shift at the reference desk. If you begin as a children's librarian or reference librarian, volunteer for collection management duties on a limited basis. These experiences help you understand the library as a connected whole instead of disparate pieces.

Getting involved in national, state, and regional library associations is invaluable to you even at the beginning of your career. Even on your entry-level salary. These associations keep you informed about the library and information world, especially budget trends and financial issues.

Chapter 4

Necessary Skill Sets

Both acquisitions librarians and library directors need an understanding of resource management processes. Accordingly, this chapter emphasizes the skill sets necessary for materials management, including budgeting; initiating acquisition activity through collection development; working together as a team; communicating and maintaining workflow for firm orders; performing the licensing/contract work that supports ordering; and understanding the procurement and accounting systems that perform the acquisition of resources. In addition, this chapter addresses the standard practices of acquisitions such as approval plans, continuations, standing orders, and the components of serials workflow that sustain acquired resources, as well as the life cycle of acquiring electronic resources.

To the extent possible, the skills sets presented in this chapter are grouped together to represent their sequential relationships. However, as many of these activities are ongoing and even recursive, it is not possible to arrange all of them in a perfect consecutive order. The first group of skills involves identifying relevant and desirable resources for the collection; the concepts of collection development, teamwork, and communication are covered here. The second category of skills connects processes that should be understood and internalized conceptually. The processes discussed include the workflow components for print acquisitions, such as approval plans, firm orders, continuations, standing orders, and serials. Included within this second category of skills is the ability to create diagrams and flowcharts to represent these processes and cycles. A third skills category involves the externally created processes with which acquisitions librarians and staff need to comply. Librarians need to understand license/contract procedures, their institutions' procurement systems, and the life cycle of electronic resources. The fourth and final category involves the reciprocal skills of accounting and budgeting. These require quantitative ability, classification, research, estimation, and forecasting. An analysis of each skill set follows.

Collection Development, Teamwork, and Communication

Collection Development

The collection development process depends on multiple perspectives working together to allocate available resources among the clearest collection needs. This aim is generally best served by a committee structure that includes librarians who interact with patrons, vendors, and the collection. The following discussion represents a case study of a collection development committee's progress in an academic library, but it should closely reflect the collection development process in other environments as well.

The committee considers how to spend available budget monies in light of the needs of constituents (which are departments and students, in the case of an academic library), taking input from the reference and instruction librarians. The committee often finds itself in a situation where it must decide how to spend "end-of-year" money on curriculum-supporting resources in a short amount of time, generally from mid-April to mid-May. In order to accomplish this task, the leader of the collection committee must manage a list of ongoing/unfilled needs as well as maintain a prepared group of preresearched potential electronic resources to present for discussion. The committee determines the priorities for procurement through consensus. The prioritized list is called the "wish list."

Generally, the collection management committee does not use end-of-year money for subscribed content. The typical philosophy regarding end-of-year money is that this money should represent a lasting investment for the university instead of a benefit limited by the time constraints of subscription. A decade ago, this philosophy meant that acquisitions assistants frantically ordered over $100,000 of books during the last month of the year. These days this philosophy translates to perpetual access to digitized monograph and ephemera collections and perpetual access to back files of scholarly journal collections. Collection management committees would not consider using end-of-year money to pay for a year's subscription to any database or journal title.

The collection development committee and the acquisitions librarian have an increasingly important responsibility—the assessment and evaluation of the library's portfolio of resources compared against the undergraduate and graduate curricula and the research needs of faculty. This evaluation depends on information gathered from several sources—meetings with faculty, university general education committee meetings, requests by students, and collaboration with the assessment librarian who sits on the university curriculum committee. On occasion, the committee decides to deselect ongoing electronic resources based on factors gleaned in the evaluation phase. In these instances, the acquisitions librarian cancels the resource with the vendor and documents the decision in the acquisitions module of the integrated library system (ILS).

To provide enhanced assessment data, the acquisitions module of the ILS is configured so that each resource is linked to the department and degree program it supports. Resources spent to support new faculty members each year are also tracked in the acquisitions module as such and associated with the correct department and individual. These links occur as a result of library staff combining funds and order codes in the system. Using the "Create List" function, the acquisitions librarian can create reports that list journal titles, continuations, and monographs for each department in order to solicit feedback from faculty. In the previous ILS, technical services librarians approximated book expenditures on behalf of a department by selecting monograph order records based on Dewey Decimal Classification (a poor match to university department).

Prior to this ILS implementation, acquisitions relied on a subscription agent for journal reports associated with fund codes, primarily associated with print journal titles. In the past year, the acquisitions librarian collaborated with the assessment librarian and the serials librarian to identify each title that we pay for within the major electronic journal packages (Elsevier, Emerald, Oxford) and to designate each title by a department and level of program support: "PhD," "Masters," "Undergraduate," "Courses, [No degree]," "[No courses]." The title becomes associated in the system with the department and the degree it supports.

This process improves over designating titles that we paid for through our subscription agent because it allows us to allocate costs to journals based on usage. For journal titles that are added in "big deal"-type packages, where the added title may not have been part of the historical subscription nor retain perpetual access rights, the department budget does not incur charges. These titles have an order amount of zero even though they are associated with the specific department fund and program. Assessment librarians can, for the first time, target every title that supports a particular program for accreditation, whereas in previous years they had to list everything that was in a package whether it was relevant or not.

Now the collection assessment librarian or acquisitions librarian can provide a department chair or faculty library liaison with a list of everything subscribed to or purchased on behalf of the department. The list includes information about the costs associated with those titles, which titles a department benefits from but is not charged for because of participation in "big deals" (such as Elsevier's Science Direct), and the potential budget impact of dropping one title in order to add another.

Teamwork

A librarian tasked with budget or acquisition responsibilities works very closely with coworkers in technical services. If the librarian also serves as a director, then human resources becomes involved on a daily basis as well. In small libraries, the director may frequently interact with all employees and many patrons. In my library, in the technical services department, consultation (three or four emails and at least one in-office conversation) occurs every day between the serials librarian and the acquisitions librarian about specific details of titles, coverage, usage, licensing issues, and how to represent a title in our ILS as an order type, as a status, etc. The same type and degree of consultation occurs between the assessment librarian and the acquisitions librarian about eBook licensing, eBook procurement, faculty requests for unusual or expensive print items, and faculty requests for electronic resources (such as a single component or item) that require special acquisitions handling. In addition, these two librarians frequently confer and experiment with how to measure our investment and usage in electronic resources using our ILS (with such functions as "Create Lists," "Access Databases," "Web Management Reports," for example). The serials librarian and the monograph cataloger confer daily about consistent representation in the catalog. Approximately three times per week, one or more of these librarians discuss with the ILS systems administrator how to resolve emerging issues. The same ILS systems administrator responds to questions and technical difficulties from technical services staff daily.

When new issues emerge, whether technical (such as a new system or technology) or personnel (a new department position needs to be crafted), all of the collection management and technical services librarians meet to discuss all relevant points of view and allow insights to emerge as the discussion unfolds. Although finding time to meet may seem difficult, the expense of making an ill-conceived or poorly developed decision exceeds the cost of making a sound one. My colleagues have been considerate, thorough, and professional in these deliberations, and, although one cannot always claim to enjoy the depth and intensity of these meetings, overall, they help build clarity and respect for both the work and perspective of your coworkers.

Our collection development committee includes members from the reference and instruction team, librarians from the technical services area, and two members of the library's administrative council. This hybrid composition allows for better communication between librarians with different functional responsibilities.

The work of acquisitions librarians or directors tasked with budget and other financial responsibilities intricately interweaves with many other responsibilities, systems, commitments, and constituents. Active, ongoing dialogue with other librarians and staff provides communication essential to creating budgets, selecting resources, and explaining changes.

Communication: Sources and Uses

A librarian tasked with budget or acquisition responsibilities assesses every conversation with coworkers, board members, employees, and patrons for relevant information about constituents' needs, collection needs, service opportunities, and partnership opportunities. Each individual that you communicate with represents their lifeworld, described by

Husserl as the realm of original self-evidences (Carr 1970, 331–339), including the influence of other people with whom they frequently interact. Consciously or subconsciously, with every conversation each individual conveys relevant voices, experiences, and opinions of influential, unseen others to your awareness. Corporations collect volumes of information, mining transactions with their customers, in order to glean patterns and predict trends. As a librarian, your sensitivity to your community, its subpopulations, loyal patrons, and occasional visitors, provides the same valuable intelligence.

Constituent needs drive all librarians. Know your subpopulations: the true and valiant, the true and tired, the new and insecure, the immigrants who struggle to learn English, the children, the amateur genealogists, the high school researchers, the local collection of creative writers, photography hobbyists, the Civil War buffs, book clubs of all shapes and sizes, volunteers, antique collectors, gun collectors, the welcomed financial donor, and the well-meaning gift book donor. Simply by their presence, each of these people tells you something about your community and its needs. Undoubtedly, each of these individuals knows someone, a relation or friend, who does not join them when they sojourn in the library. Ask the individual "why?" Be sure to explain that you will not be offended; you just want to know. You may find out something valuable about the organization, its location, its hours, the friendliness of its staff, its parking, or its services. Ask these individuals how they arrived at the library. Did they drive themselves? Did they take public transportation? Do they work nearby? Do they visit during their lunch hours? Are they unemployed?

Board members/trustees vary in their history with the library and their commitment. If possible, try to spend time with each board member or trustee individually before meeting with them as a group. Learn about each person's likes and dislikes with regard to the library. What has his or her history been so far? How did each become a board member? What has been his or her contribution to date? Does this person actively participate in fundraising or volunteer efforts? How does board membership serve this individual's goals? This information shapes the board member's relationship with the library and with you.

In an academic library, the counterpart of the board member may be a member of the university library committee, a department chair, or a department liaison, depending on the structure of the institution. The same rules apply to these individuals as the external constituents in the discussion above. Again, try to meet with them individually and learn their specific scholarly interests. What are the strong areas of scholarship in their departments? Are there specific weaknesses in the collection that they hope to redress? Do they know of any funding sources that could help mitigate these weaknesses? Do they think that their department, as a whole, feels well served by the library's reference instruction efforts? How do they measure quality in terms of library support? What are the priorities of the department? What are their suggestions for improvements? Is the department willing to commit resources to help the library improve the service?

Employees provide important sources of information about interactions with patrons, insights into demand and trends in use, and observations regarding the pace and state of day-to-day operations. The employee often has perceptions of daily situations that supplement other analysis. Communication with employees should remain open ended and low-risk for the employee. In situations where employees may feel uncomfortable, asking them for their perspective allows employees to describe perception without being forced into a fixed judgment. In contested situations, this strategy saves individuals from having to defend a position that becomes untenable when more information comes available.

Major Resource Management Processes

Firm Orders

Firm orders represent the standard, traditional workflow for acquisitions departments. A book is requested. An acquisitions staff member orders the book from a vendor by creating a purchase order. The purchase order contains the title, author, international standard book number (ISBN), quantity purchased, and estimated price of the book. The book arrives; the acquisitions staff member compares the book received to the purchase order to make sure that the book meets the order's specifications. The vendor sends an invoice when the book is shipped. The acquisitions staff member receives the invoice against the purchase order, which closes the purchase order. The acquisitions staff requests payment by generating a voucher, attaching the invoice, and sending this documentation to an accounting assistant. The acquisitions staff member also updates the ILS to record the receipt of the expected book and sends the book to the cataloging queue.

The necessity of representing workflows visually was introduced in the beginning of this chapter An example for standard firm order workflow appears in Figure 4.1.

Understanding Continuations and Standing Orders

Continuations and standing orders have different workflows from firm orders, because, most of the time, there is no original request to the vendor or publisher for the item. Instead, the librarian and the vendor have an agreement in which the vendor sends books in a particular series, in a particular genre, or with other agreed-upon characteristics to the library each time a new work is published. If librarians already know that they need these types of works for their collection, standing orders and continuations save the time of the acquisitions staff because they do not have to place or track those orders. For instance, in my library, a standing order is in place for all children's and young adult books that win awards (such as Caldecott, Newbery, Coretta Scott King, etc.). Because these books fit the collection criteria and serve important educational goals, an arrangement is made with a book jobber that specializes in children's books to send us all the award books as part of a standing order.

Because standing order books were never requested by a specific individual, they show up in the acquisitions department without an existing request or order. When they arrive, an acquisitions assistant creates an order in the acquisitions module for each book received this

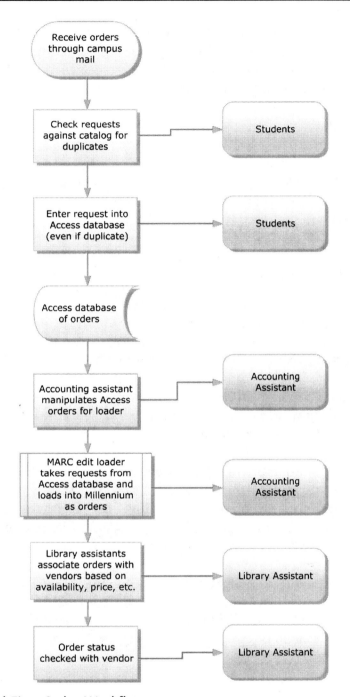

Figure 4.1 Standard Firm Order Workflow.

way. Since the book is in hand, the assistant can usually find an OCLC[1] record by searching via an ISBN. Through a library membership with OCLC, the assistant can download a copy of the cataloging record into the acquisitions system to create a bibliographic record for the item. Once the bibliographic record is created in the ILS, the assistant can create the order record, receive the item against the order, and process the invoice for that item for payment.

Continuations generally refer to a class of materials that the library receives as part of a periodic publishing cycle (such as encyclopedias, almanacs, handbooks). These materials may be published every year, every other year, or every seven years. These continuations automatically arrive at the library as a function of the publication cycle.

A third type of continuation consists of a monographic series. Monographic series are often published in volumes and note the name of the series. However, the series may include works that are not closely related to prior works in that series. In the acquisitions module, we create a master order record for that series for payment purposes only. The master order record is attached to a series bibliographic record but is suppressed in the online public access catalog (OPAC).

Approval Plans

Approval plans help the library streamline book selection by creating profiles with a vendor. The vendor then selects each title that falls within the profile criteria, ships the title to the library, and then sends the invoice. This process saves the time of librarians and other selectors while ensuring that books about specific topics are acquired.

Approval plans traditionally allow the library to return a certain small percentage of the approved books if they do not meet the library's selection standards. Generally, this percentage ranges 2–5% of the total volume.

Creating profiles for an approval plan requires knowing exactly what types of books meet the needs of constituents. In an academic library, the approval plan should support the curriculum and research needs of departments and programs within departments. Approval plans for public libraries generally target specific genres, such as mysteries, or categories, such as best sellers.

Creating approval plan profiles requires selecting among variables. The acquisitions librarian chooses specific publishers (scholarly or trade), binding (hardbound, paperback), price points (under $25.00, under $150.00, etc.), and books that fit certain classification criteria in the Dewey Decimal or the Library of Congress Classification Systems.

Approval plans have different workflows from firm orders because they do not begin with a request or an order. Figure 4.2 illustrates a semi-automated workflow in which information about approval books is downloaded from the vendor site, converted into a Microsoft Excel file, then added to a Microsoft Access database. A MARC Edit[2] loader takes the information from the Microsoft Access table and enters it into our ILS system as brief bibliographic records and attached purchase orders. When the approval books arrive from the vendor, the invoice is received against the purchase order, and the item is created and attached to the bibliographic record. The remainder of the process is just like the standard firm order process. The standard firm order workflow becomes the basis for other acquisition workflows, and other modifications are added as necessary.

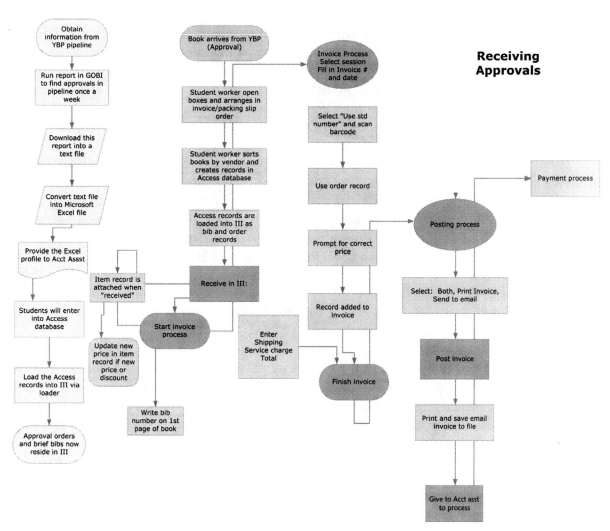

Figure 4.2 Approval Order Workflow.

Serials

Acquiring serials differs from the traditional practices of buying books. Librarians historically subscribed to serials, which meant that they paid an annual or quarterly subscription and received issues over an agreed-upon term. Because the invoice and payment process did not occur with each receipt of an issue, a separate check-in process arose to track receipts of journal and magazine volumes. Based on a title's individual pattern of publication, the library staff would create a pattern to expect upcoming issues. When the issue arrived, they would record the arrival as part of the pattern. In instances when the journal issue did not arrive in accordance with the time noted in the pattern, the library staff would note the discrepancy and file a claim with the publisher or a third-party agent managing the fulfillment role for several publishers. The agent or publisher would check their records and send the missing issue or otherwise communicate with the library about publications delays.

As journals transitioned from print publishing to electronic publishing, traditional print check-in and claiming has gradually subsided. In its place descended an avalanche of technology and procedures set up to provide access to these electronic journals through database aggregators, publishers and publisher-specific interfaces, interface technology to bridge the disparate interfaces with the OPAC, federated searching products, platforms, content management systems, and discovery systems.

Thankfully, access issues remain divorced from the accounting and acquisitions issues of periodicals, as they provide their own challenges. Librarians usually buy journals and magazines in large packages or deals directly from the publisher or through the same type of third-party agent that previously fulfilled print subscriptions. Another possibility is for journal content to be acquired through a database provider that has aggregated journal content from different publishers and combined this content into a new subscription product. Yet another possibility is that a consortium of libraries can join together, uniting their purchasing power and collectively subscribing to a combination of different aggregator products and direct publisher deals from a variety of sources. All of these possibilities have different accounting implications.

Keep in mind that in addition to the variety of different procurement processes associated with serials, the basic issue of acquiring journals differs because of the magnitude of the expense involved. Serials subscriptions often cost hundreds or thousands of dollars per title, compared to books, whose average hardcover list prices range from $15.00 to $200.00 (for an academic chemistry title, for example).

In the most direct payment process (method one), librarians pay publishers directly for annual subscriptions per title. Libraries receive annual invoices that list the titles and terms included in the subscription. This process may occur when the publisher offers an electronic journal package or individual print journal titles. In cases of electronic journals and electronic journal packages, a licensing agreement or contract usually precedes the invoice.

In the second option (method two), the librarian pays the subscription agent for the journal titles. The agent usually expects full payment several months before the beginning of the subscription term. In addition, the subscription agent charges a fee per title for the service. In this arrangement, the subscription agent acts as a clearinghouse between libraries, who subscribe to journals, and the publishers, who provide journals. The agent combines the payments and addresses and other necessary information of the subscribing libraries and provides it to the publishers. During the subscription term, the library claims all of their missing issues, regardless of title or publisher, through the subscription agent. The agent aggregates the claim information by journal title and communicates it to the publisher.

The third arrangement (method three) involves a library acquiring electronic resources through an agreement among consortia members. These situations mirror the clearinghouse model of subscription agents, in that a third party (the consortia) combines the purchasing power of its members and acts on their behalf to acquire access to subscribed electronic content for a negotiated price. In this arrangement, the consortia generally charges a fee to the member libraries to cover administrative costs. Consortia member libraries enter into the contracts and/or license agreements with the publisher. The publisher may invoice subscribing consortia libraries directly or invoice the consortia. In the second case, the consortia then reinvoices member libraries for the portion of the total cost, and when the total amount is collected, they pay the publisher's invoice.

Contracts and Licenses

Most electronic resources require licensing that protects the publisher against abusive downloading and other copyright violations. The necessity of a contract is up to the vendor. If the publisher/vendor will accept a purchase order, an institution will issue a purchase order instead of a contract to decrease the amount of paperwork and effort related to the transaction.

Important contract and license issues for electronic resources include interlibrary loan provisions, provisions for how abusive end user downloading is handled, remote access provisions, perpetual access provisions, the term dates of the contract, caps on percentage of price increases from year to year, and the amount of notice given before renewal or non-renewal of the contract or license.

Contract and license policies and procedures will vary from state to state; sometimes two similar and proximate libraries must follow different guidance. Because of the variations in interpretation and practice, this section will focus on the issues, procedures, solutions, and challenges faced by the main library of a state public institution of higher education. This example may provide other libraries with alternative processes or validating experiences.

In a typical academic year, the acquisitions department licenses and/or contracts for database content services from College Source, Emerald, Westlaw, Ebrary (now ProQuest), Bowker, Adam Matthew Digital, Elsevier, OCLC, SRDS, Oxford, ProQuest, and Alexander Street Press. Documentation that must be filed with the institution's contracts office includes the vendor's license (if no contract is required) or the contract, the Sole Source Justification Form (the same one filed with the procurement office), the Document Approval Form, and the Contract Monitoring Form.[3] When the vendor receives the signed contract/license and payment, the contract is implemented and access to the resources is granted.

The collection management department prefers to receive a copy of the signed license/contract back from the contracts office. The contract or license is scanned and stored in collection management system directory files.

Under Tennessee state law, all contracts expire after five years, so regardless of how advantageous the contractual terms are, they must be renegotiated, recontracted, and/or relicensed at least every five years. Because of the precarious funding situation in the last few budget cycles, our contract terms are limited so that the library budget remains flexible enough to cancel up to 25% of the electronic resource budget with one year's notice based on renewal lapses, if necessary. Keeping this portion of our electronic resource budget under contract terms of one year obviously means that we are repeating the same paperwork and negotiations every year. It is a tradeoff between efficiency and risk.

In the fall of 2011, the main library of a state public institution of higher education institution adopted *SERU: A Shared Electronic Resource Understanding: A Recommended Practice of the National Information Standards Organization* (NISO RP-7-2008), under specific agreements that meet university and state board of regents procurement requirements. *SERU* provides an alternative to the time-consuming and expensive use of librarians' and attorneys' time negotiating standard contracts for electronic resources between libraries and vendors who have established positive working relationships with each other and have mutually satisfied business expectations. These parties may choose to forgo license agreements and rely on the shared agreements articulated in the *SERU* document. Both publishers and libraries should be registered with the National Information Standards Organization/*SERU* registry to proceed with an agreement. Once registration of both parties is established, the library generates a purchase order instead of a license agreement (National Information Standards Organization 2012). The purchase order indicates price and subscription dates and acts as the contract for procurement purposes.

For many libraries, *SERU* eliminates the need for an annual license for all but the largest vendors. In an example of a large undergraduate university, although much of the paperwork (Document Approval Form, Sole Source Justification Form, and the Purchase Requisition Form) must still be completed, there is a clear advantage to not waiting for the licensing agreement or contract to be reviewed by the contracts office, signed by several key signatories, mailed to the vendor for signature, returned to the contracts office—all while the collection management department awaits a signed copy sent to us—the advantage is that *SERU* saves weeks of access time.

One institution's shift to *SERU* occurred because the contracts office staff met with librarians and library staff and attentively listened to suggestions for streamlining and improving the process. The serials librarian had researched *SERU* and brought documentation with her. Months later, the lead contracts attorney for the university announced she was ready to move forward with *SERU* with some stipulations.

The contracts office also customized the procurement system, SciQuest, an e-procurement software, to track the workflow of contracts through the approval process within the institution, to the vendor/publisher, and back to the institution.

Acquisitions and the Life Cycle of an Electronic Resource

Expanded access to electronic resources results in more complex and problematic acquisition and integration of such resources. A diagram illustrating the life cycle of electronic resources (Figure 4.3) follows.

Acquisitions manages the first half of the process: selection, licensing and/or contract negotiation, and payment. These three processes will be discussed in detail later in this book. Access involves providing the vendor with the appropriate internet protocol (IP) addresses (when the contract is for a site license) or passwords (for limited seat licenses), as well as obtaining from the vendor the Web address that will be used in the library's Web site for remote users. The next step in the process is to create a record for the catalog that describes the resource accurately and provides appropriate metadata; this allows the resource to be found by patrons who will search for it in future catalog searches, Web searches, or by using other discovery platforms.

The last stage of the cycle, evaluation, occurs from the time the resource becomes integrated into the collection until the collection development committee decides whether to renew the contract or select another resource.

During the term of the license, the vendor should be supplying COUNTER-compliant usage statistics for the resource. "COUNTER compliant" refers to a globally accepted standard for measuring online usage (Shepherd 2005, 287). Appropriate consideration of usage

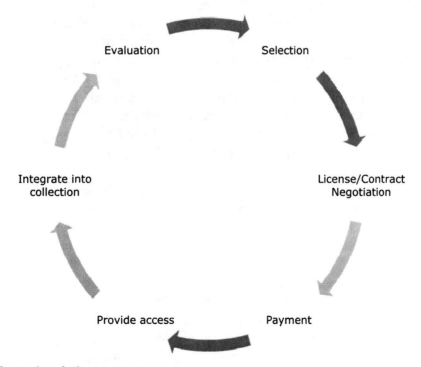

Figure 4.3 Life Cycle of Electronic Resources.

statistics for collection management depends on several criteria, the foremost of which is that a year's worth of usage statistics should be used when calculating cost per use (not just a running total of usage to date). Basic usage and cost per use should be compared within disciplines. Comparing cost per use for a large aggregator database to a subject-specific resource is not appropriate, as one type of use could not be substituted for another. These resources probably should be seen as having a complementary, not competitive relationship.

Another limitation of usage statistics is their appropriateness as a useful measure of resources acquired on a perpetual-access license. Since the term of the life cycle for the resource is, well, perpetual, then original cost plus hosting fees would need to be divided by all current, past, and future use to arrive at cost per use figures. At a minimum, do not compare cost per use of term-licensed resources with perpetual-access resources, as the ratios do not use the same base time period to measure usage.

With these limitations established, low usage points to one or more problems with the resource and should be investigated. Are there problems with access? Could the resource be better marketed among faculty in specific departments or reference librarians?

Although it does not have a place on the life cycle on Figure 4.3, tracking the renewals of electronic resources is a separate function of its own. At our library, more than one librarian and more than one library assistant may participate in this ongoing process, which involves a wiki where every license is listed with pertinent details of discussions with vendor representatives, university contract specialists, other collection management employees, and other library employees. In addition, spreadsheets record amounts and renewal dates for electronic resources for each university system (Banner) account. This spreadsheet spans several years. Email is used to communicate with each other, and these communications are archived in email folders labeled by vendor and sometimes product. The process of renewing existing resources takes tremendous amounts of staff time, because our library evaluates usage statistics on electronic journals each year and weeds out unused titles to make room for new faculty requests. These changes are made in consultation with the departments and their faculty. While the library has been fortunate to escape a large journal cancellation project in the last few years, the librarians have found it necessary to constantly churn our journal subscription collection to keep it relevant to our faculty's needs.

The life cycle diagram represents electronic journals, publisher databases, and aggregator journal databases. Although these electronic resources still engage in constant redefinition of themselves and the market, some stability has occurred. The recent emergence of patron-driven acquisitions of electronic books created the newest variations to the life cycle.

Now the stages of selection, license and contract, payment, access, and integration continue to exist, but they are not always identifiably in the same sequence as before and not (in the case of selection) always handled by librarians. Patrons select the book from within the catalog interface or OPAC without necessarily knowing if they are purchasing a book or selecting an eBook that the library already owns. Through agreements and technology, eBook vendors and the ILS companies have already created access mechanisms for eBooks.

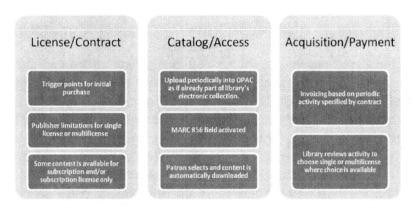

Figure 4.4 eBook Process Considerations.

Payment occurs after the patron accesses the content, in contrast to the traditional acquisition methods where payment precedes obtaining content. Figure 4.4 illustrates the electronic book process.

The vendor invoices the library monthly for eBooks that have met contractually established criteria, such as minutes of access or number of downloads. These eBooks become permanent additions to the collection.

Licensing and contracting for eBooks remain more convoluted at this time, because the original eBook companies have been acquired by bigger content providers. Currently, a library might have a contract for some of these resources through the original company and others through the new company. The complicated situation gets more difficult when eBook publishers sell through other eBook vendors, who sell through other vendors. Although the library buys books from the same vendor, these books may have vastly different license restrictions based on their publisher.

Even when the same publisher and vendor are involved, more than one licensing option exists. An electronic book may be purchased with a single license or a multiple-use license. Both licenses are perpetual use. The difference is that multiple people can check out the book simultaneously with the multiple-use license, where only one person can check out the book at a time with the single license. The multiple-use license usually costs a multiple of the list price. In 2011, Ebrary offered their multiple-use licenses at one and one-half times the list price. Not all eBooks that Ebrary offered were available for multiple or even single perpetual-access licenses.

Some publishers only contracted with Ebrary to allow Ebrary to offer their electronic books on a subscription basis. Subscription basis represents a new model in book acquisitions; although some companies did lease books to libraries in the past, it was never on this kind of scale. The state public institution of higher education used in prior examples subscribed to the eBook academic subscription. This eBook collection has high usage statistics.

Understanding the Institution's Procurement and Purchasing Systems

The procurement and purchasing office handles the acquisition of goods and services from the perspective of the institution's relationship both to its parent institution and to its external vendors. The procurement and purchasing function serves as a clearinghouse for the institution that ensures that the university/branch system/main office/government agency receives the best prices for their combined purchasing power with vendors. In addition, this office makes sure that purchases conform to the policies and procedures of the governing parent institution. In state and municipal governments, federal governments, and many private organizations, procurement and purchasing rules are formal and complex. At this state university, purchase orders are created through the purchase requisition system. Transactions processed through the procurement system (SciQuest, for example) are recorded in the institution's enterprise resource management (ERM) system (for example, Banner) using index and account codes assigned for library material accounts. The ERM system represents the external accounting system (from the perspective of the library), while the acquisitions module represents the library's internal accounting for orders, receipts, returns, and payments of resources.

The design of this system serves a factory or institution that buys commodities or "widgets" (as they say in the accounting world). "Widget" is a made-up name for any part or supply that is identical from unit to unit and shares the same price. Pencils are widgets. A particular textbook is a widget. A specific model of laptop is a widget. Basically, if an institution can buy it in bulk and get some type of bulk discount, it is a widget, no matter what it is. Purchasing and procurement systems are built for buying and accepting delivery of widgets.

Unfortunately, collecting widgets is not what librarians do. Librarians rarely buy more than one of the same item. They may buy more than one copy of a book, but that situation is rare when compared to how many books they actually buy. Even in the situation with buying classics, these are bought in slightly different editions, different imprints. The books often are different enough to have different ISBNs. Librarians buy and collect unique items. The shift towards collecting electronic content only intensifies this phenomenon. How many Elsevier Freedom Collections did your library buy last year? One, if you are fortunate. How did your procurement and purchasing system respond to that transaction? Probably as an anomaly. Many, if not most, library transactions exist outside the bounds of institutional procurement and purchasing systems. As a result, special systems and paperwork emerge to protect the institution from the risk that such a large commitment of resources and complex licensing and contractual restrictions can impose beyond the ordinary scope of the procurement and purchasing function. For example, procurement documents may include a Sole Source Justification Form, a Sole Source Letter from the Vendor, and the Purchase Requisition Form. If the amount of the contract exceeds $250,000, the contract, license, and supporting documentation must be approved by the Fiscal Review Board of the Tennessee Board of Regents.

Creating Diagrams, Flowcharts, and Mindmaps to Represent Processes and Cycles

Flowcharts need not be created at the level of a computer scientist to be useful. Your purpose is to create a drawing that represents the acquisition activities of the department in a way that is easily recognizable to other acquisitions staff and other librarians. The benefit of creating a flowchart is that it depicts your mental model of the process as you understand it. Other people can respond to the diagram and voice any concerns or differences in understanding that they may have. The flowchart that you create may help others to "see" problem areas more clearly.

A library of flowchart symbols and their definitions is provided in Table 4.1. These symbols and definitions exist within Microsoft Office Word and are easily inserted into Word documents. As long as your team agrees on the symbols and terms, you can modify these terms to create a library that best serves your purposes.

A sample of some acquisitions workflows are provided here with their libraries and definitions as examples. Drawing and discussing these flowcharts helped our acquisitions team grasp changes in workflows that resulted from implementing a new ILS system. Another flowchart software, called SmartDraw, retails for $197.00 and can be found at http://www.smartdraw.com. Figure 4.5 shows an illustrated flowchart that was created with SmartDraw.

As you create these charts, focus on one process at a time and then use the connector symbols to join these processes. It is normal for processes to connect to processes on other

Table 4.1 Library of Flowchart Symbols.

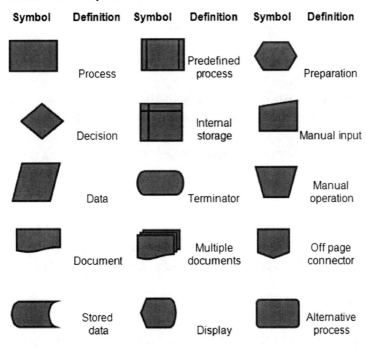

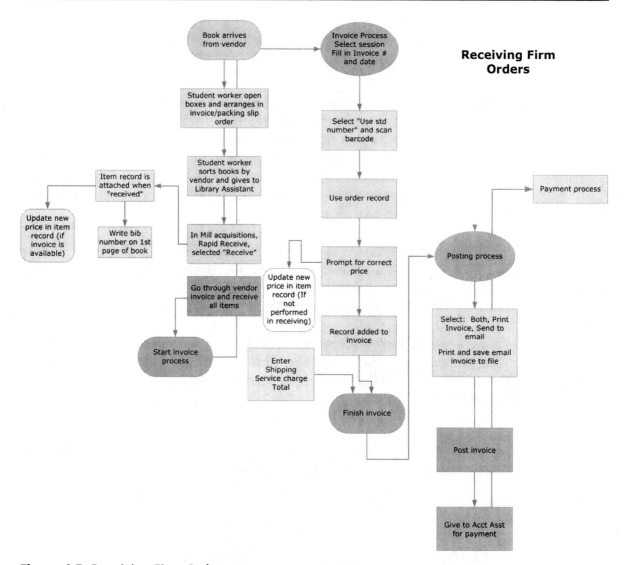

Figure 4.5 Receiving Firm Orders.

pages. In addition to the tutorials provided with the software, many tutorials exist on the Web that will help you understand the mechanics of flowcharting.

The most fundamental element of this experience is developing a familiarity with and an appreciation for the different workflows that occur in acquisitions. Firm order workflows occur any time an individual makes a request. Learn how that request is received, verified, approved or rejected, created as an order in the acquisitions module, ordered through a vendor, monitored as an order, received, paid, and transferred to cataloging. If you do not currently work in the acquisitions module, request view-only access to the acquisitions module so that you can see how each stage of the process is represented in the system.

If flowcharting works well for you, consider extending its use to your team. Flowcharts designed as a team process facilitate communication and deeper understanding of new processes or procedures, as well as build consensus about potential problem areas and solutions.

Mindmapping

A company called Inspiration Software, Inc. (http://www.inspiration.com/) specializes in visual learning tools for concept mapping, mindmapping, and creating graphs and charts. Although the software was originally developed for kindergarten through 12th grade students, Inspiration can be used to help track the big picture of projects that you are working on. Using Inspiration's software program, you choose your main idea, name other main concepts, connect these ideas together using links, and arrange them meaningfully into relationships. Concepts have many interrelationships, as illustrated by the link structure. An individual can graphically arrange these concepts in ways that make the most sense or make use of the provided graphical organizers. Inspiration allows two different displays of the data. Use the mindmap first. When you are finished, convert the mindmap into an outline. An example of both graphics follows in the mindmap illustrated in Figure 4.6.

Figure 4.6 Mindmap of Acquisitions and Collection Management Projects.

Inspiration also converts the mindmap into an outline, as shown in Figure 4.7.

Projects

I. Acquisitions

    A. Periodicals

        1. Projected periodicals budget through 6/2010

            a. Emerald Invoice

            b. Sage Invoice

            c. Elsevier

            d. Wiley

        2. Negotiate direct periodical packages

            a. Oxford

            b. Taylor & Francis

            c. University of Chicago

        3. Ebsco—check procedures

    B. Work on Wiki

    C. Book Orders

        1. NetLibrary 7th Collection

        2. Historical Statistics—TN Share deal

II. Collection Management

    A. Teach class in Estate Management for Finance Department

    B. Schedule new Collection Development Meeting

    C. SPARC databases

    D. ACM

    E. Set up Funds for PhD in Literacy Studies

    F. Assemble requests (SIAM)

    G. Talk to System Librarian about server space for purchased data sets

III. Staff Supervision

    A. Position 1—work flow analysis

        1. Wiki

    B. Position 2

        1. Job description

        2. Wiki

Figure 4.7 Outline Format of Mindmap.

Accounting and Budgeting

Accounting

Accounting is a classification system that depends on the proper recording, classifying, and interpreting of financial transactions (California Department of Finance 2005). The accounting system includes the financial statements (statement of net assets, statement of activities, etc.), the general ledger, and the accounts that comprise the general ledger (referred to as a chart of accounts). Each account in the chart of accounts flows into the general ledger. The general ledger accounts are used to create the financial statements. Accounts are carefully mapped from the lowest account level all the way up to the general ledger. The general ledger accounts are mapped to the various financial statements. Figure 4.8 illustrates how general ledger accounts relate to financial statements.

The accounting system is supported by a computer system, usually an ERM system, which tracks information and transactions across various divisions of an organization. Good accounting procedures have become increasingly essential in an environment where parent institutions face severe budget crises. Accounting is a toolbox of practices and techniques that allow librarians to track their monies carefully and effectively plan for future needs.

Budgeting

Creating a budget commits a library director, leadership team, or acquisitions librarian to a plan of action based on the organization's mission, its short- and long-term goals and resources. The mere existence of a budget is evidence of political priorities within an institution and an important tool for advocacy. A budget allocates resources to certain priorities at expense of others. Budgets clarify our needs to directors, parent institutions, the public, and so on. They become a visual aid in educating constituents about what the library does.

Budgeting and accounting have a reciprocal relationship. The California Department of Finance explains:

Both budgeting and accounting are fiscal systems or processes that involve the planning, allocating, and disbursing of monetary resources. This results in an interrelationship and a need for

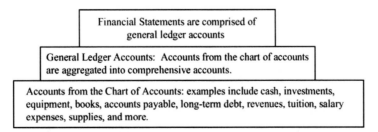

Figure 4.8 Financial Statements Built from Accounts.

coordination between these two fiscal disciplines. Generally, budgeting is regarded more in terms of planning and enacting a fiscal plan. However, these planning and enactment processes are dependent upon the accounting of past-year and current-year expenditures/revenues. (California Department of Finance 2005)

The budget embodies the financial plan for the organization, while accounting provides the measurement feedback for achieving the plan. Without an established budget that delineates (and classifies) the activities to measure, accounting just provides numbers, but not meaningful ones.

Conclusion

Acquisitions librarians need to master many diverse workflows and processes to be successful in acquiring needed resources. In addition, proper accounting and budgeting techniques require an understanding of the underlying business processes inherent in resource management. Both acquisitions librarians and library directors need to understand the processes as well as the accounting and budget measurement of these processes in order to successfully manage the financial resources of a library. If you are fortunate enough to participate in a practicum, inquire about opportunities to learn these specific skill sets.

Notes

1. OCLC is a worldwide library cooperative which shares online cataloging records. See http://www.oclc.org/au/en/about/default.htm for more information.

2. MARC Edit refers to a program developed by Terry Reese at Oregon State University. Reese decided to create an application that could function as a traditional Windows application but which also had the ability to be used and integrated with other software applications and programming/scripting languages. Reese successfully created the MARC Edit program to enable users to create MARC files out of ordinary Windows files. One application is to edit acquisitions records created in a Microsoft Access format into a MARC format and then input them into a MARC-based system. For more information, see http://oregonstate.edu/~reeset/marcedit/html/.

3. From a review of states' accounting and finance Web sites, it appears that this degree of paperwork and the insistence on justification of sole source in non-bid purchases is standard.

Section II

Accounting

Chapter 5

Generally Accepted Accounting Principles for Different Types of Libraries

Generally Accepted Accounting Principles (GAAP), comprise the minimum standards and guidelines for financial accounting and reporting and establishes appropriate measurement and classification criteria (Office of Financial Management 2001, 80.20.10). GAAP varies by type of entity (federal, state, and municipal, nonprofit and for-profit). All libraries, regardless of the type of entity they represent, are responsible and accountable to parent organizations, their board of directors, shareholders, governments, and taxpayers. In all cases, government standards determine how the library complies with the respective organization's requirements for fiscal responsibility and accountability. This chapter describes the different types of libraries and their reporting requirements, providing examples of financial statements for each type of library. Four major accounting themes will be analyzed across each library category: reporting by program, accounting for collections, accounting for investments, and the financial statement's relationship to budgets.

Many librarians may not be sure who they keep accounting records for, other than the institution-level accounting department. Chances are good that if a librarian from a private institution takes a similar position at a publically funded university, that librarian will not be aware that accounting rules differ. In fact, publically funded universities follow regulations of the Government Accounting Standards Board (GASB); private universities are regulated by the Financial Accounting Standards Board (FASB).

The way libraries relate to accounting regulatory bodies differs from how the library profession traditionally categorizes libraries (academic, public, special, K–12). Public libraries, school libraries, and academic libraries (that are part of a state, federal, or municipal government) are governed by the GASB. FASB governs the accounting practices for libraries associated with for-profit organizations such as corporate or law libraries and nongovernment nonprofit institutions.

Federal Libraries

Libraries that are part of federal agencies are governed by the Federal Accounting Standards Advisory Board (FASAB). These libraries are called federal libraries instead of government libraries (which refers to state and municipal libraries). The Federal Library Community's Web site (http://www.loc.gov/flicc/community.html) lists national libraries, cabinet-level libraries, and libraries associated with federal agencies. The National Library of Medicine, the Library of Congress, and libraries associated with federal agencies follow Federal Accounting Standards. The most authoritative source for GAAP for federal entities is contained in the *FASAB Handbook of Federal Accounting Standards and Other Pronouncements, as Amended* (*FASAB Handbook*).

The Library of Congress publishes exemplary financial statements prepared in adherence to Federal Accounting Standards. The 59-page annual report for 2010 includes 28 pages of Notes to the Financial Statements, as well as Consolidated Balance Sheets (see Figure 5.1), Consolidated Statements of Net Costs (Figure 5.2), Consolidated Statements of Changes in Net Position (Figure 5.3), and Combined Statements of Budgetary Resources (Figure 5.4; Library of Congress 2011, 18–21).

An interesting feature of the Library of Congress financial statements is in the Consolidated Statement of Net Costs (ibid., 19) where the library reports financial activity by specific program costs. The same principle is used in nonfederal government libraries such as municipal public libraries and state libraries that report their financial statements in a fund format. This format shows the reader that the Library of Congress spends most of its resources on the National Library with the Congressional Research Service following as a distant second place.

A second noteworthy item concerns the treatment of investments. The discussion of library directors' financial responsibilities introduced the topic of investment management as a component of overall library management. In the Consolidated Balance Sheet (ibid., 18), two separate categories exist for investments: one is in the category of intragovernmental, and the other is not. Both reference Note 4 of the financial statements, which explains that intragovernmental investments represent "non-marketable, market-based securities are Treasury notes and bills issued to governmental accounts that are not traded on any securities exchange, but mirror the prices of marketable securities with similar terms" (Library of Congress 2011, 32). The other (non-intragovernmental) investments are the

THE LIBRARY OF CONGRESS
Consolidated Balance Sheets
As of September 30, 2010 and 2009

	(in thousands)	
	FY 2010	**FY 2009**
ASSETS		
Intragovernmental:		
Fund Balance with Treasury (Note 2)	$ 350,417	$ 350,419
Investments (Note 4)	42,583	42,486
Accounts Receivable, Net (Note 5.A)	11,848	12,100
Other Intragovernmental Assets	1,023	225
Total Intragovernmental	405,871	405,230
Cash and Other Monetary Assets (Note 1.G)	169	104
Pledges Receivable - Donations (Note 5.B)	19,208	14,759
Investments (Note 4)	84,979	78,848
Inventory and Operating Materials (Note 1.K)	1,037	1,042
Property and Equipment, Net (Note 6)	67,015	69,138
Other Assets	544	529
Library Collections (Note 1.M)		
TOTAL ASSETS	$ 578,823	$ 569,650
LIABILITIES		
Intragovernmental:		
Accounts Payable and Accrued Funded Payroll, Benefits	$ 6,109	$ 5,966
Advances from Others	33,091	40,019
Actuarial Unfunded Workers' Compensation (Note 9)	1,756	1,657
Other Liabilities (Note 11)	130	61
Total Intragovernmental	41,086	47,703
Accounts Payable and Accrued Funded Payroll, Benefits	74,908	65,108
Deposit Account Liability	6,920	6,845
Accrued Unfunded Annual and Compensatory Leave	26,295	25,605
Actuarial Unfunded Workers' Compensation (Note 9)	7,461	6,743
Other Liabilities (Note 11)	5,291	2,795
TOTAL LIABILITIES	$ 161,961	$ 154,799
Commitments and Contingencies (Note 10)		
NET POSTION		
Unexpended Appropriations—All Other Funds	$ 199,250	$ 207,157
Cumulative Results of Operations—Earmarked Funds (Note 18)	185,214	173,519
Cumulative Results of Operations—All Other Funds	32,398	34,175
TOTAL NET POSTION	$ 416,862	$ 414,851
TOTAL LIABILITIES AND NET POSITION	$ 578,823	$ 569,650

Figure 5.1 Library of Congress Balance Sheet.

THE LIBRARY OF CONGRESS
Consolidated Statements of Net Costs
For the Years Ended September 30, 2010 and 2009

	(in thousands)	
	FY 2010	**FY 2009**
NET COSTS BY PROGRAM AREA		
National Library:		
Program Costs	$ 485,331	$ 461,909
Less: Earned Revenue	(4,351)	(4,191)
Net Program Costs	**480,980**	**457,718**
Law Library:		
Program Costs	25,477	24,986
Less: Earned Revenue	(15)	(20)
Net Program Costs	**25,462**	**24,966**
Copyright Office:		
Program Costs	81,326	73,886
Less: Earned Revenues	(38,481)	(30,033)
Net Program Costs	**42,845**	**43,853**
Congression Research Service:		
Program Costs	148,424	139,411
Less: Earned Revenue	(1)	(3)
Net Program Costs	**148,423**	**139,408**
National Library Service for the Blind and Physically Handicapped:		
Program Costs	89,401	52,032
Less: Earned Revenue	(2)	(4)
Net Program Costs	**89,399**	**52,028**
Revolving and Reimbursable Funds:		
Program Costs	110,135	101,920
Less: Earned Revenue	(94,255)	(83,446)
Net Program Costs	**15,880**	**18,474**
NET COSTS OF OPERATIONS	**$ 802,989**	**$ 736,447**

Figure 5.2 Library of Congress Statements of Net Costs.

library's investments in private sector mutual funds. Cost was derived from the investments made plus reinvested gains, dividends, and interest (ibid., 33).

A third interesting issue involves the method that the Library of Congress uses to recognize the value of its collection. See if you can find the value of the collection (look on page 18). The term "Collections" appears in the top third of the page, right above the total assets. Surprisingly, the value for "Collections" is left blank for the biggest and one of the most valuable library collections in the world. In the Notes to Consolidated Financial Statements (Library of Congress 2012, 27, 38), the section states:

THE LIBRARY OF CONGRESS
Consolidated Statements of Changes in Net Position
For the Years Ended September 30, 2010 and 20009

	Earmarked Funds	All Other Funds	Consolidated Total	Earmarked Funds	All Other Funds	Consolidated Total
CUMULATIVE RESULTS OF OPERATIONS						
Beginning Balances	$ 173,519	$ 34,175	$ 207,694	$ 177,318	$ 28,565	$ 205,883
Budgetary Financing Sources:						
Appropriations Used		642,917	642,917		588,400	588,400
Non-exchange Revenue	443		443	584		584
Donations of Cash or Securities	16,221		16,221	15,537		15,537
Transfers In/(Out) Without Reimbursement	382	(277)	105	212	(131)	81
Other	3,436		3,436	232		232
Other Financing Sources (Non-exchange):						
Donations of Property and Services	398	42,118	42,516	569	43,456	44,025
Transfers—in/out without Reimbursement	(31)	31	-			
Imputed Financing	3,719	98,991	102,710	3,231	88,835	92,066
Other	4,559		4,559	(2,667)		(2,667)
Total Financing sources	29,127	783,780	812,907	17,698	720,560	738,258
Net Cost of Operations	(17,432)	(785,557)	(802,989)	(21,497)	(714,950)	(736,447)
Net Change	11,695	(1,777)	9,918	(3,799)	5,610	1,811
CUMULATIVE RESULTS OF OPERATIONS	$ 185,214	$ 32,398	$ 217,612	$ 173,519	$ 34,175	$ 207,694
UNEXPENDED APPROPRIATIONS						
Beginning Balances	$ 0	207,157	207,157	$ 0	195,373	195,373
Budgetary Financing Sources:						
Appropriations Received	0	643,337	643,337	0	607,096	607,096
Appropriations Transferred In/(Out)	0	(1,137)	(1,137)	0	(1,851)	(1,851)
Other Adjustments	0	(7,190)	(7,190)	0	(5,061)	(5,061)
Appropriations Used	0	(642,517)	(642,517)	0	(588,400)	(588,400)
Total Budgetary Financing Sources	0	(7,507)	(7,507)	0	11,784	11,784
TOTAL UNEXPENDED APPROPRIATIONS	0	199,250	199,250	0	207,157	207,157
NET POSITION	$ 185,214	$ 231,648	$ 416,862	$ 173,519	$ 241,332	$ 441,851

Figure 5.3 Library of Congress Changes in Net Position.

THE LIBRARY OF CONGRESS
Combined Statements of Budgetary Resources
For the Years Ended September 30, 2010 and 2009

	(in thousands)	
	FY 2010	FY 2009
Budgetary Resources		
Unobligated Balance, Brought Forward, October 1	$ 1,291,000	$ 1,273,622
Recoveries of Prior-year Unpaid Obligations	34,432	21,650
Budget Authority:		
Appropriation	667,338	893,416
Spending Authority from Offsetting Collections:		
Earned:		
Collected	150,993	132,523
Change in Receivables from Federal Sources	795	179
Change in Unvilled Customer Orders:		
Advances Received	(3,808)	2,939
Without Advances from Federal Sources	(767)	3,726
Total Budget Authority	814,551	1,032,783
Nonexpenditure Transfers, Net	(1,137)	(1,851)
Temporarily Not Available Pursuant to Public Law	0	0
Permanent Not Available	(7,190)	(5,090)
TOTAL BUDGETARY RESOURCES	**$ 2,131,656**	**$ 2,321,114**
STATUS OF BUDGETARY RESOURCES		
Obligations Incurred:		
Direct	$ 1,876,804	$ 892,330
Reimbursable	164,782	137,784
Total Obligations Incurred	2,041,586	1,030,114
Unobligated Balance—Exempt from Apportionment	71,216	1,276,668
Unobligated Balance—Not Available	18,854	14,332
TOTAL STATUS OF BUDGETARY RESOURCES	**$ 2,131,656**	**$ 2,321,114**
CHANGE IN OBLIGATED BALANCE		
Unpaid Obligated Balance, Net, Brought Forward, October 1:		
Unpaid Obligations, Brought Forward	$ 278,013	$ 281,300
Less: Uncollected Customer Payments, Brought Forward	(12,492)	(8,587)
Total Unpaid Oblication Balance, Net	265,521	272,713
Obligations Incurred, net	2,041,586	1,030,114
Less: Gross Outlays	1,986,690	1,011,751
Less: Recoveries of Prior-Year Unpaid Obligations	(34,432)	(21,650)
Change in Uncollected Customer Payments from Federal Sources	(29)	(3,905)
Unpaid Obligated Blance, Net, End of Period:		
Unpaid Obligations	298,477	278,013
Less: Uncollected Customer Payments from Federal Sources	(12,521)	(12,492)
TOTAL UNPAID OBLIGATED BALANCE, NET, END OF PERIOD	**$ 285,956**	**$ 265,521**
NET OUTLAYS		
Gross Outlays	$ 1,986,690	$ 1,011,751
Less: Offsetting Collections	(147,185)	(135,462)
Less: Distributed Offsetting Receipts	(1,471)	(6,404)
TOTAL NET OUTLAYS	**$ 1,838,034**	**$ 869,885**

(The Library has no Non-Budgetary Credit Program Financing Accounts; all amounts above are Budgetary.)

Figure 5.4 Library of Congress Statements of Budgetary Resources.

The Library classifies its collections as Heritage Assets, that is, assets with historical, cultural, educational, artistic or natural significance. The Library's mission is to make its resources available and useful to the Congress and the American people and to sustain and preserve a universal collection of knowledge and creativity for future generations. ... The cost of acquiring additions to the collections is expensed, when incurred, in the statement of net cost. (27)

The Library's collections are classified as "heritage assets." $27.3 million and $25.4 million of the amount designated as "Library Materials" above represents the fiscal years 2010 and 2009 cost incurred by the Library for "heritage assets." (38)

The practice of omitting the value of the collection in the financial statements does not occur in state or municipal libraries, private nonprofit libraries, or those libraries in the private for-profit sector.

The fourth and final interesting feature of the Library of Congress's financial statements is the Consolidated Statement of Net Changes in Position, which essentially represents reporting financial activity from a budgeting point of view. Many librarians create and report financial activity based on their budgets, but few examples of this level of sophistication exist.

The four topics just discussed—reporting by specific programs, accounting for investments, accounting for collections, and interpreting financial activity through the mechanism of the budget—represent important accounting themes to be pursued throughout our examination of types of libraries.

Federal libraries are unique in that they share standard, centralized procurement, as well as acquisition and accounting policies. As of 1994, 1,234 federal libraries existed (National Center for Education Statistics [NCES] 1998, 6).[1] Federal libraries receive procurement and financial accounting support and training through the Federal Library and Information Network (or "FEDLINK"; Library of Congress 2012). Contracting officers of the Library of Congress negotiate basic contracts for library and information products or services with vendors on behalf of the federal agencies participating in FEDLINK. FEDLINK administers the contracts for the participating libraries (Federal Library and Information Center Committee 2004, 54). FEDLINK leverages the purchasing power of the federal offices participating in the program and contracts with more than 130 major vendors to provide services, saving the offices in cost avoidance benefits and in vendor volume discounts (Library of Congress 2011, 8). FEDLINK specifically provides accounting support to member libraries and regularly offers library automation and information science training for federal information professionals and technical staff. In addition, FEDLINK offers annual intensive training institutes that include acquisitions as well as ongoing online and hands-on training (Federal Library and Information Center Committee 2004, 57–58). Because of the centralized accounting systems, acquisitions practices, and consistently available training already available to federal librarians, this book will not address federal library accounting issues in the same level of depth as other types of libraries.

Private Nonprofit Organizations

Accounting for private nonprofit (nongovernment) libraries is addressed by FASB 117, The Financial Statement for not-for-profit organizations that requires: A statement of financial position, A statement of activities, A statement of functional expenses (required for voluntary health and welfare organizations and encouraged for other not-for-profit organizations), A statement of cash flows, and Financial statement disclosures. In addition to the requirement for the nonprofit entity to report the organization's total assets, liabilities, and net assets in a statement of financial position; the change in an organization's net assets in a statement of activities; and the change in its cash and cash equivalents in a statement of cash flows; nonprofit libraries must also classify their assets (materials, books, endowment accounts for collections) into several categories based on restrictions set by donors. If, for instance, an individual donated a large sum of money to endow acquisitions of books for the history department, the amount of principal for that endowment fund is classified as permanently restricted. Amounts donated to the library for general use purposes would be considered unrestricted.

> This Statement also requires classification of an organization's net assets and its revenues, expenses, gains, and losses based on the existence or absence of donor-imposed restrictions. It requires that the amounts for each of three classes of net assets permanently restricted, temporarily restricted, and unrestricted—be displayed in a statement of financial position and that the amounts of change in each of those classes of net assets be displayed in a statement of activities. (Financial Accounting Standards Board [FASB] 1993, 4)

Unrestricted assets may be expendable for any purpose that carries out the organization's mission, as they are not subject to donor-imposed stipulations. Temporarily restricted assets are subject to donor-imposed stipulations that may or will be met by actions of the organization or by passage of time. When the necessary conditions are met, temporarily restricted net assets are reclassified into unrestricted assets and reported in the statements of activities as net assets released from restrictions. Permanently restricted assets have donor-imposed restrictions that the resources remain in perpetuity. Unless otherwise stipulated, income generated by these assets may support general operating activities (FASB 1993, 8).

The National Center for Charitable Statistics at (http://nccs.urban.org/projects/ucoa .cfm) acts as the national clearinghouse of data on the nonprofit sector in the United States. In addition to providing guidance on classifying activities and programs, as well as designating regulatory reporting requirements, this organization provides a uniform chart of accounts to nonprofit organizations. This chart of accounts is provided at no cost, and it can easily transform financial statement data into categories required by the IRS and the federal Office of Management and Budget, as well as into other standard reporting formats.

An example of a sophisticated nonprofit library is prepared for you as Nonprofit Example. The Statements of Financial Position, Statements of Activities, and Statements of Cash Flows are illustrated in the next three figures.

Note the placement of "Net assets" in Figure 5.5 and the associated categories ("Unrestricted," "Temporarily restricted," and "Permanently restricted"). Over 85% of the hypothetical

June 30, 2010 and 2009

(Amounts in thousands)		2010	2009
Assets	$	$223	266
Cash			
Receivables			
Investments		5,646	3,426
Interest and dividends		369	593
Other		263	132
Investments		335,106	738,151
Investments loaned under securities lending agreement		21,620	24,073
Investments whose use is limited		461	378
Collateral held under securities lending agreement		28,221	49,692
Property and equipment, net		130,515	135,565
Collections and other assets		181,448	138,668
	$	$703,872	1,090,944
Liabilities and Net Assets			
Liabilities:			
Accounts payable	$	1,619	2,824
Payables on investment purchases		6,289	4,964
Accrued and other liabilities		21,677	18,394
Payable under securities lending agreement		14,282	23,669
Bonds payable		56,989	59,398
		100,856	109,249
Net assets			
Unrestricted		603,016	981,695
Temporarily restricted		102	92
Permanently restricted		58	59
		603,176	981,846
	$	704,032	1,091,095

Figure 5.5 Nonprofit Example, Statements of Financial Position.

library's net assets are unrestricted. The flexibility available in using net assets to carry out the mission of the organization is highly advantageous. The trust has $704 million dollars available to further its mission.

Returning to the four areas of special examination—reporting by specific programs, accounting for investments, accounting for collections, and interpreting financial activity through the mechanism of the budget—look first at the Statements of Activities in Figure 5.6, in the middle of the page, under "Expenses." The "Expense" category presents the four major programs of this hypothetical nonprofit example: Museum, Library, Preservation Institute, and Foundation. Expenses, listed in descending amounts, correspond to each program. For instance, expenses associated with the Museum program totaled $17,694,000. Had you noticed that all amounts were listed in thousands? Look at the top of the page under the title.

Are the revenues, other support, and investment income associated with the specific programs? No, these programs are supported by the general revenue and income-producing

Years ended June 30, 2010 and 2009

(Amounts in thousands)		2010	2009
Change in unrestricted net assets:			
Revenues and other support			
Sates and other income	$	3,450	3,520
Contributions		531	485
Investment loss:			
Interest and dividend income, net		4,562	8,433
Net realized and unrealized loss on investments		(357,069)	(21,388)
Net investment loss		(352,507)	(12,955)
Net realized and unrealized loss on rate swap agreements		(4,767)	(3,036)
Net assets released from restriction		296	303
Total revenues, support, and losses		(352,997)	(11,683)
Expenses:			
Program services:			
Museum		17,694	20,130
Library		4,304	6,761
Preservation Institute		2.322	4,155
Foundation		2,306	4,640
Total program services		26,626	35,686
Supporting services:			
General and administrative		1,124	1,189
Total expenses		27,750	36,875
Pension and other post retirement plans adjustments		2,059	5,317
Loss on debt extinguishment		-	(1,732)
Change in unrestricted net assets		(378,688)	(44,973)
Change in temporarily restricted net assets:			
Contributions		47	62
Net assets released from restriction		(39)	(40)
Change in temporarily restricted net assets		8	22
Change in permanently restricted net assets:			
Contributions		10	23
Change in net assets		(378,670)	(44,928)
Net assets, beginning of year		981,846	1,026,774
Net assets, end of year	$	$603,176	981,846

Figure 5.6 Nonprofit Example, Statements of Activities.

activities of the trust. If it was possible to associate revenues and income with the programs, each program would be delineated to match revenues, expenses, and the net financial impact of the program.

The hypothetical nonprofit library invests much of its money, and that investment activity shows up in both the asset and liabilities sections. In Figure 5.5, four asset categories exist for investment and investment-related receivables: "Investments," "Investments loaned under securities lending agreement," "Investments whose use is limited," and

Years ended June 2010 and 2009

(Amounts in thousands)	2010	2009
Cash flows from operating activities:		
Change in net assets		
Adjustments to reconcile change in net assets to net cash used in operating activities	(378,670)	(44,928)
Depreciation and amortization	7,739	8,239
Amortization of bond discount	30	1,222
Net realized and unrealized loss on investments	365,248	32,911
Noncash contributions of art	(398)	(292)
Loss on disposition of property and equipment	530	600
Gain on disposition of collection items	(32)	(51)
Pension-related changes	3,270	(2,361)
Contributions restricted for long-term investment	10	23
Changes in operating assets and liabilities		
Interest and dividends receivable	427	(399)
Other receivables	51	206
Other assets	31	169
Accounts payable	1,321	624
Accrued and other liabilities	79	(723)
Net cash used in operating activities:	(364)	(4,760)
Cash flows from investing activities:		
Proceeds from sales of investments		
Purchases of investments	461,928	467,961
Purchases of collection items	(458,113)	(456,353)
Proceeds from sales of collection items	(3,013)	(6,135)
Purchases of property and equipment	12	43
Proceeds from sale of property and equipment	(399)	(745)
	235	29
Net cash provided by investing activities:	650	4,800
Cash flows from financing activities:		
Proceeds from bonds payable	4,084	4,482
Payments on bonds payable	(4,423)	(4,242)
Payments on termination of swap agreement	-	(333)
Contributions restricted for long-term investment	10	12
Net cash provided by (used in) financing activities:	(329)	(81)
Net decrease in cash	(43)	(41)
Cash, end of year	266	307
Supplemental disclosure of cash flow information:	223	266
Cash paid during the year for interest	2,072	2,189

Figure 5.7 Nonprofit Example, Statements of Cash Flows.

"Collateral held under securities lending agreement." In the liabilities section, the future financial obligations are indicated by "Accounts payable," "Payables on investment purchases," "Accrued and other liabilities" (short-term debts), "Payable under securities lending agreement," and "Bonds payable" (long-term debt).

Figure 5.7 provides an illustration of the breadth of financial activities that occur at this nonprofit library throughout the year. The majority of these cash flows are related to investment activities in the nonprofit example. Many nonprofit libraries are not fortunate enough to finance most of their resources from their investment activities. The nonprofit library that you manage may have fewer categories.

This example was chosen because it illustrates relatively diverse and complex classification categories. In Figure 5.5, note the asset category for Collections and other assets for materials (books and other resources) that have been capitalized.

For-Profit Libraries

For-profit libraries include corporate libraries such as those in pharmaceutical companies, accounting firms, law firms, hospitals, and other private businesses. Like private nonprofit libraries, these libraries report their financial statements in accordance with FASB. Almost all for-profit libraries exist within a larger corporate framework. Likewise, their financial information becomes absorbed into the corporate entity's financial statements. Because very few examples of for-profit libraries exist, focus will be on the parent institution.

This example focuses on a for-profit higher education institution that provides library services to its students as part of its instructional mission. Capella University, a wholly owned subsidiary of Capella Education Company (Capella), provides an opportunity to understand financial statements of a public company. Capella Education Company's stock (symbol "CPLA") is traded on the Nasdaq Global Market, and therefore this entity must file regular financial reports with the U.S. Securities and Exchange Commission. Our analysis focuses on Capella's Form 10-K for the fiscal year ended December 31, 2010, Commission File Number: 001-33140 (Capella Education Company [Capella] 2011).

Within the Form 10-K filing, Capella describes the library services it offers as extensive learner support services (Capella 2011, 3). The extensive learner support services also include writing, tutoring, and research services; online class registration; transcript requests; financial aid counseling; and career counseling services. The Capella University Library exists as an online, virtual library that students access via a password-protected Liferay portal and content management system (ibid., 11). The online library offers a comprehensive collection of online journals and eBooks, as well as interlibrary loan services. Students communicate with librarians via email and phone to receive help with research and learning. The library offers tutorials, virtual instruction sessions, consultations on research assignments, and online research guides. Librarians also attend residential colloquia to teach library instruction sessions. Interlibrary loan services are provided through an agreement with the University of Michigan (ibid., 10).

As you read and examine the financial statements provided in Figures 5.8 through 5.11, notice the emphasis on valuation of this organization's worth to its stockholders and

	As of December 31,	
	2010	**2009**
	(In thousands, except par value)	
ASSETS		
Current assets:		
Cash and cash equivalents	$ 77,416	$ 102,405
Marketable securities	115,818	69,670
Accounts receivable, net of allowance of $3,783 in 2010 and $2,362 in 2009	13,680	12,691
Prepaid expenses and other current assets	8,290	6,564
Deferred income taxes	2,444	2,186
Total current assets	217,648	193,516
Property and equipment, net	44,910	37,984
Total assets	$ 262,558	$ 231,500
LIABILITIES AND SHAREHOLDERS' EQUITY		
Current liabilities:		
Accounts payable	$ 4,599	$ 5,027
Accrued liabilities	29,962	24,328
Income taxes payable	344	61
Deferred revenue	5,885	7,876
Total current liabilities	40,790	37,292
Deferred rent	3,466	2,952
Other liabilities	855	434
Deferred income taxes	7,838	6,556
Total liabilities	52,949	47,234
Redeemable noncontrolling interest	1,023	0
Shareholders' equity:		
Common stock, $0.01 par value:		
Authorized shares—100,000		
Issued and outstanding shares—16,306 in 2010 and 16,763 in 2009	163	168
Additional paid-in capital	115,075	151,445
Accumulated other comprehensive income	758	1,333
Retained earnings	92,590	31,320
Total Shareholders' equity	208,586	184,266
Total liabilities and Shareholders' equity	$ 262,558	$ 231,500

The accompanying notes are an integral part of these consolidated financial statements.

Figure 5.8 Capella Education Consolidated Balance Sheet.

its compliance with relevant government regulations. For-profit institutions of higher education represent a highly scrutinized industry sector. Through its financial statements, this company communicates its priorities, strategy, and profitability.

	Year Ended December 31,		
	2010	**2009**	**2008**
	(In thousands, except per share amounts)		
Revenues	$ 426,123	$ 334,643	$ 272,295
Costs and expenses:			
Instructional costs and services	164,231	135,286	120,347
Marketing and promotional	120,427	99,632	82,733
General and administrative	46,464	35,803	29,113
Total costs and expenses	331,122	270,721	232,193
Operating income	95,001	63,922	40,102
Other income, net	2,038	2,384	4,061
Income before income taxes	97,039	66,306	44,163
Income tax expense	35,860	23,637	15,375
Net income	61,179	42,669	28,788
Net loss attributable to noncontrolling interest	91	0	0
Net income attributable to Capella Education Company	$ 61,270	$ 42,669	$ 28,788
Net income per common share attributable to Capella Education Company:			
Basic	$ 3.68	$ 2.55	$ 1.71
Diluted	$ 3.64	$ 2.51	$ 1.66
Weighted average number of common shares outstanding:			
Basic	16,648	16,713	16,835
Diluted	16,848	17,030	17,322

The accompanying notes are an integral part of these consolidated financial statements.

Figure 5.9 Capella Education Company Consolidated Statements of Income.

Discussion and Analysis of For-Profit Libraries

To emphasize the continuity of important acquisitions themes despite inherent differences in entity structure and governance, Capella's financial statements are analyzed through the framework of its reporting by specific programs, accounting for investments, accounting for collections, and budget activity.

Reporting by Specific Programs

Capella Education Company includes its wholly owned subsidiary, Capella University, and a majority interest of a joint venture, Sophia Learning, LLC (Sophia). Capella (2011, 1) describes Sophia as a proprietary content provider and delivery system:

> Sophia provides a social teaching and learning platform that integrates education with technology. Sophia offers learning packets, which are small collections of academic content focused around delivering a specific subject by individual contributors. These learning packets will enable educators to supplement their teaching methods with interactive tools.

	Common Stock		Additional Paid-in Capital	Accumulated Other Comprehensive Income	Retained Earnings / (Accumulated Deficit)	Total Shareholders' Equity	Comprehensive Income
	Shares	Amount					
				(In thousands)			
Balance at December 31, 2007	17,363	$ 173	$196,643	$ 195	$ (40,137)	$ 156,874	$ 22,986
Exercise of stock options	342	3	6,153	0	0	6,156	
Stock-based compensation	0	0	4,298	0	0	4,298	
Income tax benefits associated with stock-based compensation	0	0	2,647	0	0	2,647	
Issuance of restricted stock, net	0	0	(9)	0	0	(9)	
Repurchase of common stock	(1,039)	(10)	(58,287)	0	0	(58,297)	
Net income	0	0	0	0	28,788	28,788	28,788
Unrealized gain on marketable securities	0	0	0	380	0	380	380
Balance at December 31, 2008	16,666	$ 166	$151,445	$ 575	$ (11,349)	$ 140,837	$ 29,168
Exercise of stock options	349	4	7,497	0	0	7,501	
Stock-based compensation	0	0	3,652	0	0	3,652	
Income tax benefits associated with stock-based compensation	0	0	3,620	0	0	3,620	
Issuance of restricted stock, net	1	0	(42)	0	0	(42)	
Repurchase of common stock	(253)	(2)	(14,727)	0	0	(14,729)	
Net income	0	0	0	0	42,669	42,669	42,669
Unrealized gain on marketable securities	0	0	0	758	0	758	758
Balance at December 31, 2009	16,763	$ 168	$151,445	$ 1,333	$ 31,320	$ 184,266	$ 43,427
Exercise of stock options	257	2	6,840	0	0	6,842	
Stock-based compensation	0	0	3,698	0	0	3,698	
Income tax benefits associated with stock-based compensation	0	0	4,325	0	0	4,325	
Issuance of restricted stock, net	7	0	(119)	0	0	(119)	
Noncontrolling interest contributions	0	0	(1,346)	0	0	(1,346)	
Repurchase of common stock	(721)	(7)	(49,768)	0	0	(49,775)	
Net income attributable to Capella Education Company	0	0	0	0	61,270	61,270	61,270
Unrealized loss on marketable securities	0	0	0	(575)	0	(575)	(575)
Balance at December 31, 2010	16,306	$ 163	$115,075	$ 758	$ 92,590	$ 208,586	$ 60,695

The accompanying notes are an integral part of these consolidated financial statements.

Figure 5.10 Capella Education Company Consolidated Statements of Shareholder's Equity.

	Year Ended December 31,		
	2010	**2009**	**2008**
	(In thousands)		
Operating activities			
Net income	$ 61,179	$ 42,669	$ 28,788
Adjustments to reconcile net income to net cash provided by operating activities:			
Provision for bad debts	8,744	6,972	5,225
Depreciation and amortization	18,512	14,533	12,246
Amortization of investment discount/premium	2,180	1,593	1,807
Gain realized on sale of marketable securities	0	0	(225)
Asset impairment	19	52	46
Noncontrolling interest	91	0	0
Stock-based compensation	3,698	3,652	4,298
Excess tax benefits from stock-based compensation	(4,251)	(3,463)	(2,506)
Deferred income taxes	1,354	1,315	(1,226)
Changes in operating assets and liabilities:			
Accounts receivable	(9,733)	(7,714)	(9,617)
Prepaid expenses and other current assets	(1,635)	(1,380)	1,214
Accounts payable and accrued liabilities	4,696	7,376	(7,575)
Income tax payable	5,030	3,434	9,188
Deferred rent	514	1,631	154
Deferred revenue	(1,991)	(1,619)	3,019
Net cash provided by operating activities	88,407	69,051	44,836
Investing activities			
Capital expenditures	(25,481)	(16,436)	(14,375)
Purchases of marketable securities	(60,211)	(1,030)	(74,707)
Sales and maturities of marketable securities	10,978	23,360	64,506
Net cash provided by (used in) investing activities	(74,714)	5,894	(24,576)
Financing activities			
Excess tax benefits from stock-based compensation	4,251	3,463	2,506
Net proceeds from exercise of stock options	6,842	7,501	6,156
Repurchase of common stock	(49,775)	(14,729)	(58,297)
Net cash used in financing activities	(38,682)	(3,765)	(49,635)
Net increase (decrease) in cash and cash equivalents	(24,989)	71,180	(29,375)
Cash and cash equivalents at beginning of year	102,405	31,225	60,600
Cash and cash equivalents at end of year	$ 77,416	$ 102,405	$ 31,225
Supplemental disclosures of cash flow information			
Income taxes paid Noncash transactions:	$ 29,563	$ 18,980	$ 7,455
Purchase of equipment included in accounts payable and accrued liabilities	$ 1,110	$ 1,135	$ 351
Noncontrolling interest contributions	$ 1,346	$ 0	$ 0

The accompanying notes are an integral part of these consolidated financial statements.

Figure 5.11 Capella Education Company Consolidated Statements of Cash Flows.

Table 5.1 Capella Student Enrollment as of Academic Quarter Ending December 31, 2010.

	Enrollment Number of Learners	% of Total
Doctoral	12,058	30.5 %
Master's	18,740	47.5 %
Bachelor's	8,435	21.4 %
Other	244	0.6 %
Total	39,477	100.0 %

Instead of emphasizing the separate activities of Capella and Sophia, Capella Educational Company (Capella) reports the financial activities of these entities in consolidated financial statements and focuses on their academic programs. Capella defines its major market segments in terms of its academic degree programs. Capella offers 43 academic programs (Capella 2011, 5). In Capella's 10-K report (1), the company states,

> We offer a variety of doctoral, master's and bachelor's programs in the following markets: behavioral health and human services, business management and technology, education and public service leadership. We focus on master's and doctoral degrees, with approximately 80% of our learners enrolled in a master's or doctoral degree program.

Capella reported its student enrollment by degree program as shown in Table 5.1: Capella Student Enrollment as of Academic Quarter Ending December 31, 2010 (11).

Capella's degree programs adhere to the specific standards for review of educational institutions to be recognized by the Secretary of the Department of Education. The Higher Learning Commission of the North Central Association of Colleges and Schools, a regional accrediting agency recognized by the Secretary of the Department of Education accredits Capella as well as Northwestern University, the University of Chicago, the University of Minnesota, and other degree-granting public and private colleges and universities in Arkansas, Arizona, Colorado, Iowa, Illinois, Indiana, Kansas, Michigan, Minnesota, Missouri, North Dakota, Nebraska, Ohio, Oklahoma, New Mexico, South Dakota, Wisconsin, West Virginia and Wyoming. Capella (2011, 13) explains how this accrediting agency conducts the program review process:

> These associations, or accrediting agencies, establish criteria for accreditation, conduct peer-review evaluations of institutions and professional programs for accreditation and publicly designate those institutions that meet their criteria. Accredited schools are subject to periodic review by accrediting agencies to determine whether such schools maintain the performance, integrity and quality required for accreditation.

Accounting for Investments

Capella holds significant investments in municipal tax-exempt securities ($115,118,000) and variable demand notes ($34,275,000), which they record at fair market prices, as well as cash and cash equivalents ($77,416,000). Capella keeps a high percentage of its investments in cash equivalents and marketable securities to ensure that it meets the liquidity require-ments imposed by government standards, as well as to mitigate risks associated with changes in interest rates. The Higher Education Act along with Department of Education regulations establish standards of financial responsibility that institutions such as Capella University must satisfy to participate in Title IV programs such as federal loans and Pell grants (Capella 2011, 16). The Department of Education annually evaluates institutions for compliance with specified financial responsibility standards. The standards are com-pared to line items from the institution's audited financial statements, and this way they provide financial metrics that measure an institution's capital resources, financial viability, ability to borrow (equity ratio), ability to support current operations from expendable resources (the primary reserve ratio), and to operate at a profit or within its means (net income ratio). An institution's financial ratios must yield a composite score of at least 1.5 for the institution to be deemed financially responsible without the need for further federal oversight. In the 10-K report, Capella asserts a composite score of 3.0 (ibid.). Capella does not disclose the actual calculation of these ratios.

Because of the high liquidity levels required by Higher Education Act and the Depart-ment of Education, Capella does not invest in derivative financial instruments or derivative commodity instruments. Capella states that its investment policy focuses on capital preser-vation and liquidity. According to their investment policy, all investments must have a min-imum Standard and Poor's rating of A minus (or equivalent). All of Capella's cash equivalents and marketable securities as of December 31, 2010 and 2009 were rated A minus or higher by at least one agency (Capella 2011, 55).

Capella manages interest rate risk by investing excess funds in cash equivalents and marketable securities. These bear a combination of fixed and variable interest rates based on various market indices. The risk that Capella is attempting to mitigate is a reduction of future investment income due to changes in interest rates. Potentially, Capella could suf-fer losses in principal if forced to sell securities that declined in market value due to changes in interest rates (ibid., 56).

Accounting for Library Resources and Collections

Ongoing library costs, such as salaries for library staff, subscriptions for electronic books and journals, and interlibrary loan fees, are represented in the income statement as "Instructional costs and services" expenses because these items of expense directly relate to educational services provided to Capella students (ibid., 46). From information provided about the library, it appears that Capella does not invest in print materials. If a student requires a book for an assignment, the student would borrow the resource through the inter-library loan service. In this case, books do not meet the requirements for a capitalized asset in the equipment category because Capella does not own the books. This practice differs from most of the libraries that we will discuss. Most libraries that operate under state government guidelines capitalize the cost of books as material or collections under long-term assets such as equipment.

Capella capitalizes some library costs that are associated with software that supports their virtual library. "Computer software" consists of purchased software, capitalized Web site development costs, and internally developed software. "Capitalized Web site development costs" consist mainly of salaries and outside development fees directly related to Web sites and various databases. "Internally developed software" includes qualifying salary and consulting costs for time spent on developing internal use software. Capella states that these costs represent direct labor, such as salaries and consulting costs. The costs are included in the property and equipment asset category and depreciated or amortized over their useful lives (Capella 2011, 64).

Interpreting Financial Activity through the Mechanism of the Budget

Budget information was not included in the regulatory filings with the U.S. Securities and Exchange Commission (Capella 2011); nor was it available via Capella's Web site.

Publically Supported Libraries

Instead of federal, private nonprofit, or private libraries, this book focuses on the largest group of libraries that share common accounting standards. Nonfederal government libraries, including public libraries, state libraries, school libraries (where the school is part of a municipal government), libraries within state institutions of higher education, and libraries of other state and municipal governments make up approximately 73% of libraries in the United States.[2] These libraries follow guidance provided by the Government Accounting Standards Board (GASB). These libraries operate in an atmosphere of accountability that differs from both the federal government and businesses. The Web site for the city of Philadelphia (City of Philadelphia 2012) explains:

> Governments are fundamentally different from for-profit business enterprises in several important ways. They have different purposes, processes of generating revenues, stakeholders, budgetary obligations, and propensity for longevity. These differences require separate accounting and financial reporting standards in order to provide information to meet the needs of stakeholders to assess government accountability and to make political, social, and economic decisions.

A hierarchy of authoritative literature exists which specifies how the accounting profession applies government accounting standards to determine GAAP on a case-by-case basis. GASB No. 55 states that standards which guide accounting for state and municipal entities begin with GASB Statements and GASB Interpretations, then continue with GASB Technical Bulletins, followed by AICPA (American Institute of Certified Public Accountants) Practice Bulletins that specifically apply to local government entities cleared by the GASB, and, last, the Implementation Guides published by GASB staff. If a librarian is searching for the proper treatment of an issue, he or she would start by looking for the highest level of GAAP and continue down the hierarchy until finding guidance to address the issue.

GASB Statements No. 34 and 35 address a variety of government institutions in addition to libraries, so the sections that deal with libraries are emphasized. These sections address how to classify and depreciate book expenditures and what to consider as "owned" when licensing databases and other electronic resources. The basic premise of these rules is that books and other library materials are considered assets to the institutions and not expenses. Operating costs like salaries and utilities are expenses (or expenditures in governmental accounting), while the purchase of books and other necessary library resources is treated more like an investment in the library (and the university, in my case). And this is how it should be, as purchasing library resources represents investing in the educational institution. These investments are the working assets of a knowledge organization (as in, they are put into use) and are considered assets in the institution's consolidated financial statements.

GASB Statement No. 54, "Fund Balance Reporting and Governmental Fund-type Definitions," issued in March 2009, establishes classifications based on the extent to which a government must observe constraints imposed on the use of resources it reports in government funds. These categories of fund balances include "Nonspendable," "Restricted," "Committed," "Assigned," and "Unassigned." "Nonspendable" means that the amounts are legally or contractually required to be maintained intact or not in spendable form. "Restricted" refers to amounts that are legally restricted by outside parties, constitutional provisions, or enabling legislations for a specific purpose. "Committed" refers to amounts formally set aside by the board of trustees for use for specific purposes. These committed amounts are made and can be rescinded via resolution of the board of trustees.

"Assigned" refers to resources that the director or board of trustees has resolved to spend for specific purposes and that have been formally approved and authorized by the board of trustees. "Unassigned" includes all resources that are available for any purpose within the library's mission.

An exemplary annual report containing Financial Statements, Notes to Financial Statements, and Management's Discussion and Analysis is the *Indianapolis-Marion County Public Library Comprehensive Annual Financial Report for the Fiscal Year Ended December 31, 2010* (*CAFR*). The Indianapolis-Marion County Public Library represents an unusually well financially administered public library. Its board has the authority to adopt a budget and recommend a tax levy (subject to approval by the city council). The library board issues its own general obligation bonds, subject to approval of the public by referendum. Beginning in 2009 and continuing into 2010, the Indianapolis-Marion County Public Library leveraged their proactive financial management into advocacy when the library "formed a team of public service staff, management, and Board representation to address the long-term financial sustainability of the library system" (Indianapolis-Marion County Public Library [IMCPL] 2011, 7). As legislation passed the state legislature that threatened to decrease property taxes and the resulting revenue source to the library, the team responded:

The team prepared a five-year forecast to project fund balances based on the projected circuit breaker reductions and economy. The results of the forecast indicated the need for a new revenue source and/or reductions in operating costs. In October of 2010, the Library reduced hours of service by 26% to address the shortage of tax revenue. The Library worked with elected officials and legislation was passed in 2011 that allows our fiscal body to allocate a share of the County Option Income Taxes to the Library. As we move forward into 2012, the Library will be seeking a share of this new tax source in hopes of restoring hours of service. (ibid.)

In addition, the Indianapolis-Marion County Public Library has received a Certificate of Achievement for Excellence in Financial Reporting, awarded by the Government Finance Officers Association of the United States and Canada for its *CAFR* for the fiscal year ended December 31, 2009. The *CAFR*'s Letter of Transmittal (8) discusses this achievement:

This was the 20th consecutive year that the Library has achieved this prestigious award. In order to be awarded a Certificate of Achievement, a government must publish an easily readable and efficiently organized comprehensive annual financial report. This report must satisfy both generally accepted accounting principles and applicable legal requirements.

Given Indianapolis-Marion County Public Library's continued excellence in financial reporting, its financial statements are given as an exemplar for government (nonfederal) libraries.

Indianapolis-Marion County Public Library's financial statements, beginning with the Government Wide Financial Statements (Statement of Net Assets and Statement of Activities), are shown, and then a close look is given to the Fund Financial Statements (Statement of Revenues, Expenditures, and Changes in Fund Balances—Governmental Funds; Reconciliation of the Statement of Revenues, Expenditures, and Changes in Fund Balances of Governmental Funds to the Statement of Activities; Statement of Fiduciary Net Assets—Fiduciary Funds; and Statement of Changes in Fiduciary Net Assets—Fiduciary Funds) (Figure 5.12–Figure 5.17).

Accounting Themes (Reporting by Program, Accounting for Collections, Accounting for Investments, and Interpreting Financial Activity through Budget Reporting)

As in the examples with federal and private libraries, an examination is given here to how the finances of public libraries "work," through the information provided in the financial statements and their accompanying notes. The financial statements of our public library example present some of the most complex accounting issues that we have addressed so far. Many of the difficult concepts are discussed in the notes section of the statements.

Reporting by Specific Program

Public libraries and state libraries must report government-wide financial statements and fund financial statements. The fund financial statements group related accounts that

INDIANAPOLIS-MARION COUNTY PUBLIC LIBRARY
STATEMENT OF NET ASSETS
December 31, 2010

Assets	Primary Government	
	Governmental Activities	Component Unit
Cash and cash equivalents	$ 26,008,055	$ 705,852
Investments		4,896,215
Receivables		
Accounts	21,088	-
Intergovernmental	800,508	-
Miscellaneous	1,552,005	-
Inventories	-	6,022
Prepaid expense	137,364	7,726
Beneficial interest in assets held by others	-	(48,982)
Restricted assets:		
Cash and cash equivalents	7,834,343	941,501
Investments	-	4,337,319
Receivables (net of allowances for uncollectibles):		
Contributions from assets held by others	-	5,767,095
Contributions from unitrusts	-	375,785
Pledges	-	1,402,523
Deferred debits	549,471	-
Contract advance receivable	299,000	-
Capital assets:		
Land, artwork, rare books, and other special collections	8,922,418	-
Other capital assets, net of depreciation	152,901,580	125,992
Net pension asset	681,057	-
Total assets	199,736,889	18,517,048

The notes to the financial statements are an integral part of this statement.

Figure 5.12 Indianapolis-Marion County Public Library Statement of Changes in Fiduciary Net Assets.

maintain control over resources that have been segregated for specific activities. Reporting by fund allows these libraries to report by specific programs. Public libraries and other government (nonfederal) libraries report these related, grouped accounts (funds) using fund accounting, which focuses on the short-term inflows and outflows of spendable resources as well as the balances of these resources at the end of the fiscal year. To understand how public libraries report by specific program, we need a basic understanding of fund accounting.

Funds

Governments report their general funds and other major funds. Government funds are the operating funds of the government. To conduct operations, a library needs cash and operating resources.

INDIANAPOLIS-MARION COUNTY PUBLIC LIBRARY
STATEMENT OF NET ASSETS
December 31, 2010

	Primary Government	
Liabilities	**Governmental Activities**	**Component Unit**
Accounts payable	1,526,201	25,072
Accrued payroll and withholdings payable	584,785	-
Contracts payable	770,837	-
Unearned revenue	134,399	-
Other current payables	-	23,324
Liabilities payable from restricted assets:		
Interest payable	2,140,179	-
Noncurrent liabilities:		
Due within one year		
General obligation bonds payable	5,730,000	-
Compensated absences	702,879	-
Due beyond one year		
General obligation bonds payable	96,817,158	-
Compensated absences	761,452	-
Deferral of loss on refunding	(573,874)	-
Other postemployment benefits	196,469	-
Total Liabilities	108,790,485	48396
Net Assets		
Invested in capital assets, net of related debt	59,276,840	125,992
Restricted for:		
Capital projects	5,765,592	-
Debt service	4,076,686	-
Foundation:		
Expendable	-	6,839,313
Nonexpendable	-	5,984,910
Unrestricted	21,827,286	5,518,437
Total net assets	$ 90,948,404	$ 18,468,652

Figure 5.12 (Continued)

GASB (2006, 33) defines (government) funds as

self-balancing sets of accounts that are maintained for governmental activities. Financial statements of governmental funds are prepared on the modified accrual basis of accounting and the current financial resource flows measurement focus.

Based on GASB's definition, the fund is not a legal entity. It is only an accounting entity which records financial transactions and can be used to track monies related to its purpose.

Like many other governmental entities and their departments, libraries use both a fund structure and an account structure that mirrors the university's general ledger.

INDIANAPOLIS-MARION COUNTY PUBLIC LIBRARY
STATEMENT OF ACTIVITIES
For the Year Ended December 31, 2010

| | | Program Revenues | | | Net (Expense) Revenue and Changes in Net Assets | |
| | | | | | Primary Government | Component Unit |
Functions/Programs	Expenses	Charges for Services	Operating Grants and Contributions	Capital Grants and Contributions	Governmental Activities	Library Foundation
Primary government						
Government activities:						
Culture and recreation	$ 42,713,697	$ 2,606,820	$ 932,335	$ -	$ (39,174,542)	$ -
Interest on long-term debt	4,945,235	-	-	-	(4,945,235)	-
Total governmental activities	47,658,932	2,606,820	932,355	-	(44,119,777)	-
Total primary government	$ 47,658,932	$ 2,606,820	$ 932,355	$ -	(44,119,777)	-
Compnent unit:						
Indianapolis-Marion County Public Library Foundation, Inc.	$ 2,392,179	$ 265,511	$ -	$ 1,633,692		(492,776)
General revenues:						
Property taxes					35,407,096	-
Intergovernmental taxes					8,668,220	-
Grants and contributions - not restricted					-	1,343,336
Other general revenues					420,590	-
Unrestricted investment earnings					179,791	704,962
Donated capital assets					796,909	-
Total general revenues					45,472,606	2,048,298
Change in net assets					1,352,829	155,522
Net assets—beginning (as restated)					89,593,575	16,913,130
Net assets—ending					$ 90,946,404	$ 18,468,652

The notes to the financial statements are an integral part of this statement.

Figure 5.13 Indianapolis-Marion County Public Library Statement of Activities.

INDIANAPOLIS-MARION COUNTY PUBLIC LIBRARY
STATEMENT OF REVENUES, EXPENDITURES, AND CHANGES IN FUND BALANCES
GOVERNMENTAL FUNDS
For the Year Ended December 31, 2010

	General	Bond and Interest Redemption	Construction	Rainy Day	Other Governmental Funds	Total Governmental Funds
Revenues						
Taxes	$ 32,291,386	$ 6,563,481	$ -	$ -	$ 702,081	$ 39,556,948
Intergovernmental	7,385,943	671,621	-	-	486,644	8,544,208
Charges for services	194,882	-	-	-	1,094,580	1,289,462
Fines and forfeits	1,397,704	-	-	-	-	1,397,704
Other	643,348	5,101	58,861	79,997	3,028,715	1,532,717
Total revenues	$ 41,913,263	$ 7,240,203	$ 58,861	$ 79,997	$ 5,312,020	$ 52,321,039
Expenditures:						
Current:						
Culture and recreation	28,868,013	-	991,523	590,854	2,207,699	32,678,089
Debt service:						
Principal	1,590,000	4,285,000	-	-	-	5,875,000
Interest and fiscal charges	1,303,137	2,868,020	-	-	-	4,171,157
Bond issuance costs	-	192,150	-	-	-	192,150
Capital outlay	4,283,500	-	94,561	-	122,341	4,500,402
Total expenditures	36,064,650	7,345,170	1,086,084	590,854	2,330,040	47,416,798
Excess (deficiency) of revenues over (under) expenditures	5,848,613	(104,967)	(1,027,223)	(510,857)	698,675	4,904,241
Other financing sources (uses):						
Refunding bonds issued	-	23,630,000	-	-	-	23,630,000
Payment to refunded bond escrow agent	-	(25,049,078)	-	-	-	(25,049,078)
Premium on sale of bond	-	1,611,991	-	-	-	1,611,991
Total other financing sources and uses	-	192,913	-	-	-	192,913
Net change in fund balances	5,848,613	87,946	(1,027,223)	(510,857)	698,675	5,097,154
Fund balances - beginning	8,477,032	(4,605)	5,413,888	6,819,459	2,722,337	2,342,811
Fund balances -ending	$ 14,325,645	$ 83,341	$ 4,386,665	$ 6,308,602	$ 3,421,012	$ 7,439,965

The notes to the financial statements are an integral part of this statement.

Figure 5.14 Indianapolis-Marion County Public Library Statement of Revenues, Expenditures, and Changes in Fund Balances—Governmental Funds.

INDIANAPOLIS-MARION COUNTY PUBLIC LIBRARY
RECONCILIATION OF THE STATEMENT OF REVENUES,
EXPENDITURES, AND CHANGES IN FUND BALANCES OF GOVERNMENTAL FUNDS
TO THE STATEMENT OF ACTIVITIES
For The Year Ended December 31, 2010

Amounts reported for governmental activities in the Statement of Activities are different because:

Net change in fund balances -total governmental funds (Statement of Revenues, Expenditures, and Change in Fund Balances)	$ 5,097,154
Governmental funds report capital outlays as expenditures. However, in the Statement of Activities the cost of those assets is allocated over their estimated useful lives and reported as depreciation expense. This is the amount by which capital outlays exceeded depreciation in the current period. (see Note II B).	(5,054,378)
Revenues in the Statement of Activities that do not provide current financial resources are not reported as revenues in the funds (See Note II B).	(4,239,229)
The issuance of long-term debt (e.g., bonds, leases) provide current financial resources to governmental funds, while the repayment of the principal of long-term debt consumes the current financial resources of governmental funds. Neither transaction, however, has any effect on net assets. Also, governmental funds report the effect of issuance costs, premiums, discounts and similar items when debt is first issued, whereas these amounts are deferred and amortized in the Statement of Activities. This amount is the net effect of these differences in the treatment of long-term debt and related items (see Note II B).	5,569,070
Negative net pension obligations and other postemployment benefits, including the Public Employee's Retirement Plan and Postemployment Healthcare Plan, are considered a net asset and obligation, respectively, of the general government and, therefore, are not reported as current expenditures in the funds (see Note II B).	(146,788)
Some expenses reported in the Statement of Activities do not require the use of current financial resources and, therefore, are not reported as expenditures in governmental funds (see Note II B).	127,000
Change in net assets of governmental activities (Statement of Activities)	$ 1,352,829

The notes to the financial statements are an integral part of this statement.

Figure 5.15 Indianapolis-Marion County Public Library Reconciliation of the Statement of Revenues, Expenditures, and Changes in Fund Balances of Governmental Funds to the Statement of Activities.

All government entities covered by GASB use at least a general fund. The library may only maintain one fund and, if so, it is the general fund. The general fund accounts for all revenue and expenditures necessary to operate and provide service for a library.

Other government funds include special revenue funds, debt service funds, capital projects funds, and endowment funds/permanent funds. Special revenue funds account for the proceeds of earmarked revenue or financing activities requiring separate accounting because of legal or regulatory provisions. Debt service funds account for the annual payment of principal, interest, and expenses in connection with certain long-term debt via

INDIANAPOLIS-MARION COUNTY PUBLIC LIBRARY
STATEMENT OF FIDUCIARY NET ASSETS
FIDUCIARY FUNDS
December 31, 2010

	Private-Purpose Trust Fund	Agency Funds
Assets		
Cash and cash equivalents	$ 582,136	$ 117,043
Receivables (net of allowance for uncollectibles):		
Accounts	-	10,650
Total assets	582,136	127,693
Liabilities		
Accounts payable	9196	$ 2,897
Payroll withholdings payable		124796
Total liabilities	9196	$ 127,693
Net Assets		
Held in trust for the Indianapolis-Marion County Public Library Foundation, Inc.	$ 572,940	

The notes to the financial statements are an integral part of this statement.

Figure 5.16 Indianapolis-Marion County Public Library Statement of Fiduciary Net Assets.

special voted property tax levies or transfers from other funds. Often, the use of debt service funds is optional. Capital projects funds account for the development of capital facilities, such as an addition to a building, and are typically established for the construction of fixed assets or to set aside money for future capital needs. The last category includes endowment funds/permanent funds. Endowment funds account for gifts and bequests that may be either

INDIANAPOLIS-MARION COUNTY PUBLIC LIBRARY
STATEMENT OF CHANGES IN FIDUCIARY NET ASSETS
FIDUCIARY FUNDS
December 31, 2010

Additions	Private-Purpose Trust Fund
Contributions:	
Private donations	$ 686,898
Investment income:	
Interest	808
Total additions	$ 687,706
Deductions	
Educational outreach	482,696
Change in net assets	205,010
Net assets - beginning	367,930
Net assets - ending	$ 572,940

The notes to the financial statements are an integral part of this statement.

Figure 5.17 Indianapolis-Marion County Public Library Statement of Changes in Fiduciary Net Assets.

expendable or nonexpendable, depending on legal restrictions that apply. Permanent funds represent a new category (used to report resources that are legally restricted to the extent that only earnings, not principal) that may be used for purposes that support the reporting government's programs. Permanent funds report trust arrangements in which the reporting government is the beneficiary, including public-purpose funds previously classified as nonexpendable trust funds.

Indianapolis Marion County Public Library reports by fund. Government funds represent the primary type. Government funds provide information on near-term inflows, outflows, and balances of spendable resources (IMCPL 2011, 20). The library maintains 11 individual governmental funds. Information for governmental funds is presented separately in the governmental fund statement of revenues, expenditures, and changes in fund balances (Figure 5.14). The governmental fund statement of revenues, expenditures, and changes in fund balances focuses on the major funds such as the general fund, the bond and interest redemption fund, the construction fund, and the rainy day fund. The data from seven other library governmental funds are combined into a single, aggregated presentation. The individual fund data for these nonmajor governmental funds appears in pages 63–64 of the annual report.

The major governmental fund, the general fund, acts as the chief operating fund of the library (IMCPL 2011, 20). By analyzing the revenue, expenditures, and changes in fund statement, you can see that the fund balance of the library's general fund, excluding transfers, increased by $5,849 during the 2010–2011 fiscal year. The general fund specifically tracks revenues and expenditures related to their culture and recreation program. The revenues for this program include tax revenue, fines and fees, and charges for services. At the end of fiscal year 2010, approximately 68% of this total amount, or $19,323, constitutes unreserved fund balance, which is available for spending at the library's discretion. The remainder of fund balance is reserved to indicate that it is not available for new spending because it has already been committed to encumbrances of $9,202 (IMCPL 2011, 17).

Investments

The Indianapolis Marion County Public Library cites an Indiana state statute (IC 5-13-9) as authorizing the library to invest in securities (2011, 41). The library may invest in federal government securities and other securities that are fully backed by the United States of America and issued by the United States Treasury, a federal agency, a federal instrumentality, or a federal government-sponsored enterprise. These investments must have a stated final maturity of less than two years. The library is also funded by a separate foundation, which as a nongovernment nonprofit participates in other investing activity on behalf of the library. The foundation reports under FASB standards, including FASB Statement No. 117, Financial Statements of Not-for-Profit Organizations. Because the foundation is allowed to participate in more diverse investments, the library benefits by having a portfolio of investments that include Cash equivalents, Certificates of deposit, Corporate bonds, Mutual funds, Equities, and Alternative investments (IMCPL 2011, 42). See Figure 5.18 for an analysis of investments at estimated fair market value.

Investments consist of the following
at December 31, 2010:

Cash equivalents	$ 779,186
Certificates of deposit	590,076
Corporate bonds	970,144
Mutual funds	2,830,878
Equities	2,651,803
Alternative investment	1,411,447
Total	$ 9,233,534

Investment returns consist of the following for the year
ended December 31, 2010:

Dividends and interest	$ 174,095
Less investment fees	(40,640)
	133,455
Realized gains (losses) on investments	128,530
Unrealized gains (losses) on investments	571,433
	699,963
Total	$ 833,418

Figure 5.18 Indianapolis-Marion County Public Library Notes to Financial Statements, Note IV. A. 1.3.

Fair market value is based on a hierarchy of measurement criteria. The first measurement is based on unadjusted quoted prices for identical assets or liabilities in active markets. If that valuation is not available, then quoted prices for similar assets or liabilities in active markets which are observable for the asset or liability either directly or indirectly provide the basis for the fair market valuation. The last category consists of valuations derived from valuation techniques in which one or more significant inputs or significant value drivers are unobservable (IMCPL 2011, 42–43). Indianapolis Marion County Public Library reports these valuations in the Notes to Financial Statements section of the *CAFR* as shown in Figure 5.19.

Investment income is reported as revenue in the operating statement (IMCPL 2011, 34).

Collections

As in the Statements of Financial Position for the example of the nonprofit library, Indianapolis Marion County Public Library (see Figure 5.20: Capital Assets; IMCPL 2011, 46) capitalizes the collection as part of fixed assets along with artwork and rare books and other special collections. These assets are reported at their historical cost (the price originally paid to acquire the work) as Total Assets, with a separate category for accumulated depreciation disclosed and subtracted from Total Assets, resulting in Net Assets for the Fixed Asset category (24). This Net Assets number ($161,824,000) equals the Statement of Net Assets category for Capital Assets (27).[3]

Following is a summary of financial assets measured at fair value in the Statements of Financial Position and the respective levels to which the fair value measurements are classified within the fair value hierarchy at December 31, 2010:

Assets:	Carrying Amount at December 31	Quoted Prices in Active Markets for Identiical Assets (Level 1)	Significant Other Observable Inputs (Level 2)	Significant Other Unobserv-able Inputs (Level 3)
Investments	$ 9,233,534	$ 6,851,943	$ 2,381,591	$ -
Beneficial interest in assets held by others	5,718,113	-	-	5,718,113
Beneficial interest in charitable remainder trusts	375,785	-	-	375,785
Totals	$ 15,327,432	$ 6,851,943	$ 2,381,591	$ 6,093,898

The following is a summary of changes in assets with significant unobservableinputs (Level 3) for the year ended December 31, 2010

	2010		
	Beneficial Interest in Assets Held by Others	Beneficial Interest in Charitable Remainder Unitrusts	Total
Beginning balance:	$ 5,255,361	$ 375,785	$ 5,631,146
Deposits	-	-	-
Investments return, net	555,752	-	555,752
Distributions	(93,000)		(93,000)
Ending balance	$ 5,718,113	$ 375,785	$ 6,093,898

Figure 5.19 Indianapolis-Marion County Public Library Notes to Financial Statements, Note IV. A. 1.4.

A complete schedule of all capital assets (including collections) and the changes to these assets from the prior fiscal year is found on (IMCPL 2011, 46) and reproduced below in Figure 5.20.

Interpreting Financial Activity through Budget Reporting

The library board of the Indianapolis Marion County Public Library has the authority to adopt the budget and recommend a tax levy to support it, but the City County Council must approve both. The budget provides the framework for the library's financial planning and control. The board must adopt a budget for the general fund, the capital projects fund, and the debt service fund by August 31 for the next fiscal year (IMCPL 2011, 6). The *CAFR* for 2010 supplies budgetary comparison schedules for the general fund (59) and the rainy day fund (61) in the required supplementary information. This information is found below. Budget information is also provided for the capital project fund (66), and bond and interest redemption fund (65) to demonstrate compliance with the fund.

Capital asset activity for the year ended December 31, 2010, was as follows:

	Beginning Balance (Restated)	Increases	Decreases	Ending Balance
Primary Government				
Governmental activities:				
Capital assets, not being depreciated:				
Land	$ 6,119,939	$ -	$ -	$ 6,119,939
Artwork	2,010,770	198,265	5,200	2,203,835
Rare Books & Other Special Collections	-	598,644	-	598,644
Total capital assets, not being depreciated	8,130,709	796,909	5,200	8,922,418
Capital assets, being depreciated				
Buildings	153,125,099	-	-	153,125,099
Improvements	2,744,856	-	-	2,744,856
Machinery and equipment	7,810,047	263,284	169,987	7,903,344
Collections	26,017,720	4,130,337	4,365,940	25,782,117
Totals	189,697,722	4,393,621	4,535,927	189,555,416
Less accumulated depreciation for:				
Buildings	13,489,716	3,030,863	-	16,520,579
Improvements	633,759	164,321	-	798,080
Machinery and equipment	4,448,605	574,495	145,486	4,877,614
Collections	12,377,974	6,445,528	4,365,939	14,457,563
Totals	30,950,054	10,215,207	4,511,425	36,653,836
Total capital assets, being depreciated, net	158,747,668	(5,821,586)	24,502	152,901,580
Total governmental activities capital assets, net	$ 166,878,377	$ (5,024,677)	$ 29,702	$ 161,823,998

Figure 5.20 C. Capital Assets.

In addition, the *CAFR* also reports reconciliations between the amounts recorded in the financial statements and the budget in the Management's Discussion and Analysis section (IMCPL 2011, 23).

The budgetary highlights section gives the reader an overview of how the budgeted revenues and expenses of Indianapolis Marion County Public Library were impacted as a result of management decisions to reduce costs. In the Letter of Transmittal, the library's management explained how the library arrived at making these budget decisions. Due to a change in legislation that would reduce tax revenues to the library, management created a budget team which projected fund balances based on a five-year forecast. The results of the forecast indicated the need for either new revenue sources and/or reductions in operating costs.

General Fund Budgetary Highlights

Differences between the original budget and the final budget resulted in a decrease of $801. This decrease along with other adjustments was distributed among the following budget classifications:

- $336 decrease in personnel services (salaries & fringe benefits).

- $24 decrease in supplies relating to a reduction in cost from our main office supply vendor.

- $30 increase in other services and charges due to an increase in snow removal at various branch locations.

- $1,008 decrease in capital outlay for our collection due to the Circuit Breaker legislation.

- $537 increase in interest expense due to a reallocation of debt payments from the debt service fund to the operating fund.

Actual expenditures were $4,597 (11 %) less than the amended final budget for 2010. The majority of the difference (41 %) was due to lower spending in personal services from hiring freezes and reduced hours of service. In addition, 25% less was spent on collection materials - books, DVD's and CD's due to the Circuit Breaker legislation.

During the year, revenues exceeded expenditures, excluding other financing uses, by $12,606, resulting in an increase in the fund balance for 2010.

The library had to reduce hours of service by 26% to address the projected shortage of tax revenue (IMCPL 2011, 7). The library is currently lobbying to recapture the lost tax revenue.

Indianapolis Marion County Public Library represents a large and complex library system. Its financial activities require significant accounting expertise, and its financial schedules need to be read in the context of its required supplemental information, management discussion and analysis, and the notes to financial statements.

If you were a librarian or director at Indianapolis Marion County Public Library or one of the other organizations that were analyzed (the nonprofit example, Library of Congress, Capella), you would work with or for financial experts in the organization who would bear the greater share of responsibility for these statements. You would not be expected to create or maintain this level of accounting sophistication. The examples in this book are meant to illustrate the goal of good accounting techniques and practices so that you understand how your activities lead to the publication of these statements.

In the following chapters, the process will begin from the opposite direction. The starting point will be intermediary accounting processes such as compiling and verifying information and back to the daily responsibilities of classifying and recording financial transactions.

Notes

1. While 1994 seems out of date, federal libraries have fairly stable lives.

2. The percentage of government libraries was computed using the total number of public libraries provided by IMLS, the number of libraries in public schools provided by NCES, and the number of academic libraries associated with public institutions of higher education provided as a percentage of the estimated total number of libraries (121,785) per ALA Fact Sheet 1 (http://ala .org/tools/libfactsheets/alalibraryfactsheet01).

3. Net Capital Assets in the Statement of Net Assets are displayed as Capital assets:

Land, artwork, rare books, and other special collections	8,922,418
Other capital assets, net of depreciation	152,901,580
Total Capital assets equals	161,823,998

Chapter 6

The Philosophy of Accounting and How Transactions Are Measured

Both the accounting and librarian professions wrestle with ambiguities inherent in providing information that faithfully represents its meaning in a manner useful to the reader. Raber (2003, 6) describes how the fundamental work of information scientists is to "identify, collect, organize and make accessible in logical and intelligible ways the textual record of human experience." This description of information science work applies to the work of accounting as well, with one caveat. The textual record of human experience becomes the transactional record of an organization's experience. The transactional record *is* a type of textual record that differs from other textual records, in that it measures and expresses activity in specifically prescribed language and calculations. Other types of textual records include data sets, computer code, as well as literary text.

In framing financial accounting concepts within the context of librarianship, you are provided with a conceptual framework for translating library events into accounting transactions and back, as well as strengthening your confidence in your judgment and ability to assess library activities from an accounting perspective. The most important quality of information (accounting and other types) is the context in which it will be interpreted. Sensitivity to context drives the questions that librarians use to communicate financial (and other types of) information: Who needs this information? And for what purposes?

To address the contextual nature of financial information, the accounting profession developed a conceptual framework that is officially promulgated in the FASB *Statement of Financial Accounting Concepts No. 8* (2010). The *Statement of Financial Accounting Concepts No. 8* identifies the objectives of financial reporting and describes the necessary qualitative characteristics of accounting information. These fundamental concepts provide a base for interpreting and applying accounting principles:

> The conceptual framework is a coherent system of interrelated objectives and fundamental concepts that prescribes the nature, function, and limits of financial accounting and reporting and that is expected to lead to consistent guidance. It is intended to serve the public interest by providing structure and direction to financial accounting and reporting to facilitate the provision of unbiased financial and related information. (FASB 2010, 2)

The objective of accounting is to provide objective, useful information much like a library collection strives to provide useful information to the public. Information centers and specialists have accepted the premise that objectivity is an ideal and not a practical standard. As such, the American Library Association (ALA) advocates balance in a collection and transparency of sources as practices that protect the user against bias. The ALA *Library Bill of Rights* asserts that books and other resources should not be excluded because of the origin or views of their creators. Instead, libraries should provide materials and information which represent all perspectives on both current and historical issues. Resources should neither be included nor excluded because of partisan or ideological disapproval (ALA 1996).

The *Statement of Financial Accounting Concepts No. 8* states that the objective of financial information is to provide information that is useful to existing stakeholders in making decisions about providing resources to an entity (FASB 2010, 1).

While librarianship would likely embrace the important responsibility of providing useful information to stakeholders, the mission of our profession expands upon the accounting concept and aims to educate, to entertain, and to create community (ALA 1996, Statement I). The librarian's adage of preparing information for the greatest benefit of the user still appears to be the most important principle. In recording accounting transactions and preparing financial reports, librarians should keep in mind the specialized information needs of these users.

Financial information users seek to know the entity's economic resources and claims against the reporting entity as well as the effects of transactions and other events that affect the reporting entity's economic resources and claims. The users want information sufficient to enable them to assess the entity's needs for additional financing and how likely it is to obtain additional financing, as well as how future cash flows will be distributed among those who claim resources against the entity (FASB 2010, 3). In short, what does this entity have, and what does it owe? The behavior of the entity over a time period evinces itself in the relationship between transactions that increase its ownership or indebtedness. The focus of government funds is to measure current financial resources, not profit. There are two basic methods to account for funds: the modified-accrual basis and the accrual basis.

The way financial transactions are measured and recorded depends on when those transactions occur, even if those resulting cash receipts and payments occur in a different period. Recording the transactions for the same fiscal time period as the underlying transaction occurred or "matching" revenues and expenses is considered the matching principle in accounting.

The focus of government funds is to measure current financial resources, not profit. As stated above, the two basic methods of accounting for funds are the modified-accrual basis and the accrual basis. Under the accrual basis of accounting, revenue is recorded when earned and expenses are recorded when incurred. In general, governmental libraries use the modified-accrual basis of accounting in the day-to-day accounting records and budgets. The full accrual basis of accounting is used to prepare the year-end financial report to be consistent with government-wide financial statements on the full accrual basis of accounting.

The matching principle forms the basis of accrual accounting. Under the accrual basis of accounting, revenue is recorded when earned and expenses are recorded when incurred. Full accrual basis of accounting is used to prepare the year-end financial report to be consistent with government-wide financial statements on the full accrual basis of accounting. For example, the purchase of a computer or library computer program would be charged as an expense at the point of the transaction if the library were not using accrual accounting (cash basis accounting instead of accrual accounting). However, using accrual accounting, the librarian would record the computer equipment as an asset and recognize the expense of the computer equipment over the years that it is used. In this method, a portion of the expense continues to be recognized over the useful life of the computing equipment. If the equipment is expected to last five years, the librarian would recognize one-fifth of the expense each year under accrual accounting using a technique called depreciation. An example of recording the purchase of computer equipment using both the cash basis and the accrual method follows.

The point of the example in Table 6.1 is to illustrate how purchasing computer equipment is divided out into two parts in accrual-based systems. In one part, the entity pays the vendor (steps 1 and 3). In another part, the expense is recognized as the equipment is used (step 2).

Accrual accounting principles are modified slightly in nonprofit institutions. In general, public and governmental libraries use the modified-accrual basis of accounting in the day-to-day accounting records and budgets. What does modified-accrual accounting mean for

Table 6.1 Acquisition of Computer Equipment Using Cash Basis vs. Accrual Accounting.

	Debit	Credit
Cash Basis		
Computer Equipment	$ 5,000	
Cash		$5,000
Accrual Basis		
Computer Equipment	$ 5,000	
Accounts Payable		$5,000
(1) To record initial acquisition of computer equipment:		
Depreciation Expense—Computer	$ 1,000	
Accumulated Depreciation—Computer		$1,000
(2) To recognize the expense of the computer equipment one year at a time as the equipment is used (Total cost of equipment divided by useful life in years = $5,000/5 years = $1,000):		
Accounts Payable	$ 5,000	
Cash		$5,000
(3) To actually pay the vendor. This transaction could occur in separate steps as in the vendor is paid $100 a month until the debt is completely paid instead of paying the whole cost at once. Important Note: this transaction only affects the statement of net assets. It has no impact on revenues or expenses.		

libraries? The *Library of Michigan Financial Management Reference Guide* (1.2–1.3) outlines the following characteristics of modified accrual accounting:

Expenditures are recorded when incurred (i.e., when the goods are received or the services rendered), not when cash is paid or when an invoice is received. Special rules are provided for the following:

- Prepaid expenses: Purchases that benefit more than one period (such as insurance paid in advance) may be prorated (but typically are not) between periods.

- Interest on long-term debt should be counted on the due date of the debt.

- Employee compensated absences (e.g., sick and vacation pay) should be counted when the amount comes due for payment, i.e., time is taken off, or the employment is terminated (note: prior to the adoption of GASB 34, compensated absences are to be recognized if paid shortly after year end, generally within 60 days).

- Contingent liabilities (e.g., lawsuits) should also be recorded at the time they come due for payment. (Michigan Department of Education 2002)

What qualifies as revenue for public libraries, which typically do not "sell" products or services to patrons? Public libraries receive revenue from various sources: taxes, fines and forfeitures, charges for services, intergovernmental transactions, and other sources. Taxes come in the form of property, sales, and income taxes. Late fines and lost book fees represents another source of revenue, and intergovernmental transactions could include federal grant monies. Generally, revenue is realized when the underlying exchange has occurred under the accrual method. Resources also should be available if modified accrual is used.

So not only must taxes be levied, but they must also be collected and available for the tax revenue to be recognized. The specific event related to the revenue has occurred and the revenue must be collected under the modified-accrual method. The modified-accrual method is more conservative than the standard accrual method. The standard accrual method recognizes revenue when it is earned, not necessarily received.

In the case of government-mandated nonexchange transactions (the receiving of funds without a "sale"), revenues are recognized when resources are received or when all eligibility requirements have been met (whichever comes first). In the case of government grants, entitlements, and donations, all eligibility requirements must be met.

Fundamental qualitative characteristics of useful financial information include relevance, materiality, and faithful representation. Additional enhancing qualitative characteristics of such information include comparability, verifiability, timeliness, and understandability (FASB 2010, 16–21).

The fundamental characteristics—relevance, materiality, and faithful representation—are essential to the usefulness of information reported in financial statements as well as other financial reports (16). Relevance in financial information is defined as the quality of being capable of making a difference in the decisions made by users. Relevant financial information may have either predictive value, explanatory value, or both (17). Materiality is the quality of significance, defined by the nature or magnitude of an item of financial information in comparison to the entity's financial report as a whole. That is to say, the inclusion or exclusion of a material item could influence the user's assessment of the entire financial statement. Faithful representation is achieving the maximization of completeness, neutrality, and accuracy for the depiction of each and all financial phenomena represented in the financial statements (17–18). Information must be both relevant and faithfully represented to be useful.

The qualities of comparability, verifiability, timeliness, and understandability enhance the usefulness of financial information. The *Statement of Financial Accounting Concepts No. 8* describes comparability as the quality that "allows information about a reporting entity to be more useful if it can be compared with similar information about other entities and with similar information about the same entity for another period or another date" (19). Comparability enables users to identify and understand similarities and differences among items. The concept is related to consistency in that comparability requires consistent methods for the same items from period to period within a single reporting entity or in a single period among more than one entity to make sense. Comparability requires consistency, but it cannot be reduced simply to consistency, because slightly different methods may be necessary to faithfully represent the same financial events that occur in different contexts. Nor does comparability equal uniformity. Forcing unlike items to look the same does not enhance the usefulness of the information (19–20).

Verifiability helps assure users that the information faithfully represents the underlying economic phenomena that it claims to represent. For information to be verifiable, different knowledgeable and independent professionals could reach consensus, although not complete agreement, about how the information is best presented to the user Verification can also occur through direct observation or indirect testing of inputs to a model, formula, or other technique and recalculation of the outputs using the same methodology (20).

Timeliness means having financial information available to decision makers in time for them to make informed decisions. In general, information loses its usefulness over time (ibid.).

The last quality of useful financial information is understandability. Understandability depends on classifying, characterizing, and presenting information clearly and concisely (ibid., 21). This definition states a concept that librarians understand intrinsically, that simplifying complicated information can backfire if the user is not provided all of the essential details.

> Some phenomena are inherently complex and cannot be made easy to understand. Excluding information about those phenomena from financial reports might make the information in those financial reports easier to understand. However, those reports would be incomplete and therefore potentially misleading. (ibid.)

After emphasizing the similarities between the goals of librarians and accountants both in providing useful information and in creating access to it, the next step is to obtain guidance on applying these qualities to financial information created by librarians on behalf of the library. The next section focuses on accounting techniques.

Chapter 7

Connecting Library Activities to Financial Performance Using Basic Accounting Practices

How are the everyday purchasing and accounting activities that were described in Section I connected to the financial statements prepared in accordance with generally accepted accounting procedures illustrated in Section II? In this chapter, you will learn basic accounting concepts that support the financial statements as well as how these concepts relate to each other.

Accounting includes classifying, recording, summarizing, and reporting of an entity's financial transactions in compliance with generally accepted accounting principles (Commonwealth of Virginia, Office of the Comptroller 2007, 4).

Basic Accounting Concepts: Classifying, Recording, Summarizing, and Reporting

The policy and procedure guidance provided by Virginia to its state institutions outlines the basic objectives of the accounting function:

Each transaction reflects correct data, including monetary amounts. Each transaction is recorded once, and only once. Each transaction is properly classified to support summarization. Summarization processes accurately reflect the underlying dollar amounts and accounting classifications. Documentary evidence exists for every accounting process. Documents enable accountants to follow an "audit trail" through the accounting process from each transaction to appropriate reports and other output. (ibid., 5)

Recording and Summarizing

An extremely important point made by the Virginia Department of Accounts emphasizes maintaining a trail that connects the same transaction through different systems. The Virginia documentation explains,

> If recorded in multiple accounting systems, transactions can be traced from one system to another, any variance between accounting data can be traced to specific transactions, and all variations are explained and justified. (ibid.)

As stated in Section I, accounting is a classification system which includes the financial statements (statement of net assets, statement of activities), the general ledger, and the accounts that comprise the general ledger (referred to as a chart of accounts). Each account in the chart of accounts flows into the general ledger, but they are often aggregated into larger categories. The general ledger accounts are used to create the financial statements. Accounts are carefully mapped from the lowest account level all the way up to the general ledger. The general ledger accounts are mapped to the various financial statements.

Figure 7.1 illustrates how accounts combine into larger account sets to create financial statements.

The accounting system is supported by a computer system, usually an enterprise resource management system (ERM) that tracks information and transactions across various divisions of an organization. Banner and SAP are ERMs widely used in institutions of higher education and state and municipal governments. The Banner finance module houses all the accounts used by the entire organization in its chart of accounts. The library will use only a portion of those accounts, and those accounts will likely have index codes that specify their use by the library.

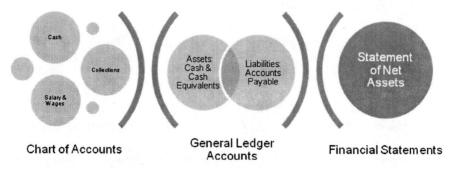

Chart of Accounts   General Ledger Accounts   Financial Statements

Figure 7.1 Chart of Accounts, General Ledger Accounts, Financial Statements.

Note that the library accounts are part of the larger organization's chart of accounts, and all of the accounts are combined to create the general ledger of the organization. The general ledger accounts form the basis for the financial statements of the organization, which are provided to state or municipal government agencies that govern the institution.

The accounts that matter to an acquisitions librarian include those for books and materials. These are usually found in the Asset class for Equipment or other capital asset accounts, because these materials are considered depreciable assets of the institution like computers and furniture.

If you are a director of a public library, the accounts that matter to you will include not only those related to material purchases, but also other Asset accounts that include accounts receivable (for fines and fees owed to the library), Liability accounts (for payments owed to vendors), Revenue accounts (charges for services, operating grants, donations, property taxes, state grants, and potentially investment returns), and Expense accounts (related to salaries and benefits, supplies, maintenance expenses for the building, utilities, debt service, and depreciation).

Recording and Classification

A transaction must be properly classified to be correctly reported. Classification requires the economic essence of the transaction and the proper codification of the transaction according the entity's financial system. The *Library of Michigan Financial Management Reference Guide* makes an intriguing analogy about the chart of accounts:

> A chart of accounts is an organized listing of all accounts used by a library to record financial information in its general ledger. The chart of accounts is to the accounting function what the Dewey Decimal System is to a library. It provides a foundation for arranging financial data into useful information. To provide reliable and consistent financial information, it is imperative that the chart of accounts be simple and functional. (Michigan Department of Education 2002, 1.9)

A simplified example of a chart of accounts for a general ledger is shown in Table 7.1.

Table 7.1 A Chart of Accounts for a General Ledger.

Balance Sheet Accounts		Balance Sheet Continued	
Assets		**Liabilities**	
1000	Cash Account	2000	Accounts Payable
1010	Petty Cash	2100	Matured Interest Payable
1020	CD Investment	2110	Matured Debt Payable
1030	Cash with Fiscal Agent	2200	Due to Other Funds
1100	Taxes Receivable-2009	2300	Working Capital Advance Due to General Fund

(*continued*)

Table 7.1   (Continued)

Balance Sheet Accounts		Balance Sheet Continued	
1110	Taxes Receivable-2010	2400	Long Term Loans Payable
1120	Taxes Receivable-2011	2500	Bonds Payable
1130	Due from Other Funds	**Fund Balance Accounts**	
1140	Working Capital Advance	2900	Fund Balance-Beginning
1150	Interest Receivable	2910	Restricted Funds
1200	Accounts Receivable	2920	Unrestricted Funds
1210	Loans Receivable	2930	Temporarily Restricted-Funds
1220	Fines and Fees Receivable	2999	Income over Expenses-Current Year
1230	Allowance for Doubtful Accounts	**Revenues and Expenditures**	
1240	Interest Receivable-Treasury Loans	**Revenues**	
1250	Accrued Interest Earned-Treasury Loans	4000	Property Taxes
1260	Equity Pooled Resources	4010	Book Fines and Fees
1270	Securities Held in Escrow	4020	Grants-Federal
1280	Funds Held in Escrow	4030	Grants-State
1290	Investments-Other	4040	Grants-Non-restricted
1295	Investments-Bonds	4050	Donations
1299	Short Term Investments	4060	Dividend/Interest Income
1300	Accrued Interest Purchased	**Expenditures**	
1310	Investments with Trustees	5000	Salaries
1400	Construction in Progress	5010	Benefits
1410	Land	5020	FICA Tax
1420	Buildings	6000	Rent
1425	Accumulated Depreciation-Buildings	6010	Utilities
1430	Infrastructure	6020	Depreciation
1435	Accumulated Depreciation-Infrastructure	6030	Loss on Investments
1440	Equipment		
1445	Accumulated Depreciation-Equipment		
1450	Collections		
1455	Accumulated Depreciation Collections		
1470	Fund Equity in Cash		
1480	Receipts in Process		
1490	Transfers in Process		
1500	Clearing Account- Cash Reconciliation Items		
1510	Other Assets		
1520	Prepaid Items		

Table 7.2 Categories of Accounts.

Assets	Owned resources
Liabilities	Debts and legal obligations
Fund Balance	Fund balance at end of fiscal year
Revenues	Income from taxes, fines, fees, etc.
Expenditures	Outflow of resources

The immediate goal includes obtaining a basic understanding of the accounts and what financial information belongs to which account. The most comprehensive categories are Assets, Liabilities, Fund Balance, Revenues, and Expenditures. Table 7.2 describes the nature of these categories.

The librarian responsible for accounting needs to be able to use the chart of accounts in Table 7.3 to record standard entries. Sophisticated accounting transactions will always require professional accounting assistance.

Standard entries made to these accounts include: buying library materials, paying staff, receiving revenues, paying for utilities, paying for supplies, and paying for equipment. These are broad categories of payments, but they should be addressed by the general ledger accounts.

These standard entries are illustrated in Table 7.3, the standard entry table. The left-hand side of the entry is called the "Debit" and is noted as "(DR)". The right-hand side of the entry is called the "Credit" and is noted as "(CR)." Use the chart of accounts in Table 7.1.

Table 7.3 Standard Entry Table.

Transaction	Accounts	Debit (DR)	Credit (CR)
1. Buying library materials (Bought and received books and now owe the book vendor)	1450 Collections 2000 Accounts Payable	$50.00	$50.00
2. Paying staff*	5000 Salaries 5010 Benefits 5020 FICA 1000 Cash	$6,000 $2,000 $1,000	$9,000
3. Receiving revenue (Federal grant money is received)	1000 Cash 4020 Federal Grants	$3,000	$3,000
4. Paying for supplies	6015 Office Supplies	$30.00	$30.00
5. (Bought printing paper on credit)	2000 Accounts Payable		
6. Paying utilities (electricity, water)	6010 Utilities 1000 Cash	$100.00	$100.00

*Remember to use payroll service to handle all of the detailed transactions and only record one entry to the ledger per pay period.

This relatively simple level of accounting becomes more complex when the library must add program and organization codes to accounting transactions. These codes allow the librarian to parse the original entry into different subgroups based on reporting needs. The Commonwealth of Virginia's Department of Accounts mandates that each transaction have a general account code (like the ones just reviewed in Table 7.1), a general fund code, and a detail fund code.

Each side of the transaction has the following format:

Account Code–Fund Code–Detail Fund Code

For example, 1450-30-40 translates to Collections–Children–Games, where we have assigned the fund code "30" to children and the detail fund code "40" to games. These extra code numbers assist librarians in breaking out which materials were purchased for the children's collection.

The amount of flexibility that your organization has depends on your parent organization. Even if your parent organization's chart of accounts is rigid, your library can account for costs at a more detailed level by using subledgers.

Subledgers, as the name suggests, record all of the detail for the major account and have the same account balances. These subledgers provide more flexibility in capturing data that you might find useful but which do not have a place in the formal account structure. Fixed assets (such as computer equipment) and Resource material collections (books, DVDs) frequently use subledgers.

Material budgets are often tracked by a subledger. Generally this subledger of funds lives within the acquisitions module of the integrated library system (ILS). Within the acquisitions module, one might have a fund for Popular Reading, for instance. At the beginning of the year, that fund would be allocated a budgeted amount for the year, and during the year the money would be spent out of the fund.

Within the ILS acquisitions module, the following transactions would occur:

1. When an order is placed and the purchase order is created in the system . . .

Encumbrance to Popular Reading Fund	$50.00	(Debit)
Popular Reading Fund Allocation	$50.00	(Credit)

2. When the order arrives, is received in the system, and is invoiced . . .

Expenditure of Popular Reading Fund	$50.00	(Debit)
Encumbrance of Popular Reading Fund	$50.00	(Credit)

An encumbrance is created when you have ordered material. The encumbrance functions as a reminder that the cost of that material is set aside and should not be considered part of your available funds. When the material arrives and is paid, the encumbrance is reversed out and no longer has any impact on the acquisitions subledger/module's fund.

It is important to realize that you do not need to make these entries. Your ILS is doing these automatically as part of the acquisitions process. These transactions provide an understanding of how fund accounting principles go on behind the scenes.

In addition to the examples provided by public libraries, an academic library may find it useful to use funds to demonstrate accountability in using resources to support specific programs, such as a specific degree program (bachelors of science in nutrition), grant program (adult literacy in a public library), or other constituency-based initiative that chooses to measures its specific costs in addition to general operating activities. We will discuss this application of funds that support the materials account when we discuss the acquisitions module and the materials account subledger.

Chapter 8

Reporting

Creating the Ledger in the Acquisitions Module

Acquisitions modules in many integrated library systems (ILSs) allow the librarian to set up as many funds as needed, but these systems differ in terms of how the funds are constructed. Some systems allow funds to be hierarchical, meaning that funds can be nested within other funds. So when you are building your ledger, it is imperative that you think carefully about how you structure the hierarchy. The hierarchy of the ledger should mirror your reporting needs as closely as possible. Do you need to know how much you spent on specific programs more often than you need to know what types of formats have been acquired or encumbered?

Your parent organization often drives your reporting needs. Figure 8.1 is an example of a ledger in which funds were structured by college/department/degree/format. The structure of the ledger facilitates reporting activities in a university library where accreditation reports require that each academic program show how much money was spent for library materials for that program each year, divided up by format (books or periodicals).

An example of this type of fund would be a master-level fund for a college (College of Liberal Arts), department (English), degree level (doctoral), and format (periodicals). This type of hierarchical fund would look like this:

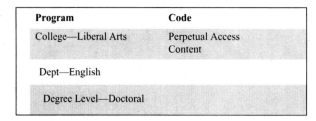

Program	Code
College—Liberal Arts	Perpetual Access Content
Dept—English	
Degree Level—Doctoral	

Figure 8.1 Fund Structure.

In this hierarchy, expenditures could be easily tracked at the college level (all departments, all degree programs, and all formats) or at the department level (all degree levels and all formats). However, if you wanted information about how much money you had either spent or encumbered for materials in periodical format for doctoral programs, you would have to create a query that asks your system for "College —Liberal Arts, Dept—*English*, Degree Level—Doctoral, Format—Periodicals" + "College—Liberal Arts, Dept—*History*, Degree Level—Doctoral, Format—Periodicals" + "College—Liberal Arts, Dept—*Art*, Degree Level—Doctoral, Format—Periodicals" + "College—Sciences, Dept—*Biology*, Degree Level—Doctoral, Format—Periodicals" + all of your other colleges and departments where periodicals were acquired to support doctoral programs. In essence, you would have to go back to the module and create a report that gathered up all of the periodical funds from all of the hierarchies where they were nested.

A public library might budget by its major constituencies: adults, seniors, children, and/or young adults. An example of a hierarchical budget is seen in Table 8.1.

However, the acquisitions ledger would include only the appropriations, expenditures, encumbrances, and the remaining balances for library materials.

Note that in this table (Table 8.1) subledger, the expenditure amounts are equal no matter what level of hierarchy you view. The totals for the major level, detail level 1, and detail level 2 all equal $213,000. Each additional hierarchical level simply provides more detail.

Other ILSs do not provide a hierarchical structure of funds in the acquisitions module. These funds exist in a flat structure only, and a hierarchy must be created to support every level of reporting. These hierarchies are created by individually identifying and including the funds desired.

Table 8.2 shows a flat fund ledger structure. The highlighted agribusiness fund has a column for its original budget appropriation, expenditure, encumbrance, free balance, and cash balance. Expenditures represent the amount paid to date. Encumbrances represent resources that have been ordered to support the agribusiness program but are not yet received. The free balance represents the cash balance minus the encumbered amount. The free balance and the cash balance are shown side by side to let the viewer assess how much of the appropriation is still available.

Table 8.1 Hierarchical Subledger for Children's Programs.

Program	Major category	Detail category 1	Detail category 2	Subtotal Major	Subtotal Detail category (1)	Subtotal Detail category (2)
Children						
	Salaries					
		Salary-Librarian			60,000	
			Salary			45,000
			Benefits			15,000
		Salary-Assistant			25,000	25,000
	Subtotal Salaries			85,000		
	Materials					
		Books			70,000	70,000
		Magazines			12,000	12,000
		Games			10,000	
			Board Games			1,000
			Video Games			9,000
		Educational Kits			5,000	5,000
	Subtotal Materials			97,000		
	Equipment					
		Computers			12,000	12,000
		Chairs			4,000	4,000
		Bookshelves			9,000	
			Short			2,000
			Medium			3,000
			Tall			4,000
		Puppet Stage			6,000	6,000
	Subtotal Equipment			31,000		
	Total			**$ 213,000**	**$ 213,000**	**$ 213,000**

Table 8.2 Flat Fund Ledger Structure.

Funds	Activity	Adjustment				
	Appropriation	Expenditure	Encumbrance	Free Balance	Cash Balance	
Accounting	$43,151.00	$54,847.33	-$37,019.34	$25,323.01	-$11,696.33	
Aerospace	$9,800.00	$10,951.07	-$764.80	-$386.27	-$1,151.07	
Agribusiness	$36,510.00	$33,443.78	$446.19	$2,620.03	$3,066.22	
Approval Economics	$15,000.00	$9,744.81	$110.00	$5,145.19	$5,255.19	
Approval English	$15,000.00	$14,748.66	$0.00	$251.34	$251.34	
Approval Gen Wks	$8,000.00	$5,048.56	$0.00	$2,951.44	$2,951.44	
Approval Health	$5,000.00	$2,839.42	$0.00	$2,160.58	$2,160.58	
Approval History	$15,000.00	$18,379.78	$0.00	-$3,379.78	-$3,379.78	
Approval Lib Awards	$3,000.00	$2,159.62	$0.00	$840.38	$840.38	
Approval Literacy	$5,000.00	$3,139.68	$0.00	$1,860.32	$1,860.32	
Approval Math Sci	$5,000.00	$743.09	$1,067.00	$3,189.91	$4,256.91	
Approval Nursing	$5,000.00	$766.59	$0.00	$4,233.41	$4,233.41	
Art	$9,700.00	$5,900.29	-$27.40	$3,827.11	$3,799.71	
Biology	$339,300.00	$311,584.01	-$33,671.08	$61,387.07	$27,715.99	
Business Com	$4,200.00	$3,477.14	-$121.87	$844.73	$722.86	
Chemistry	$470,900.00	$419,129.67	-$41,444.72	$93,215.05	$51,770.33	
Comp Info Sci	$18,730.00	$12,191.28	$3,398.29	$3,140.43	$6,538.72	
ComputationalSci	$5,000.00	$6,709.55	-$3,448.00	$1,738.45	-$1,709.55	

Table 8.3 Approval Fund Hierarchy.

In book acquisitions, many book orders will come in under list price because of vendor discounts, or orders may not be filled because of limited print runs. Discounts cannot be applied until the item is actually received. Therefore, the free balance is usually slightly understated. Acquisitions librarians consider the available money to spend as an estimate between the free balance and the cash balance.

The following tables illustrate a fund hierarchy created to monitor approval programs set up to support specific programs. Table 8.3 shows the hierarchy. Table 8.4 shows the way the grouped funds display.

The fund information from the approval hierarchy in Table 8.3 allows us to monitor the performance of the approval plan. The approval plan for history exceeds its original budgeted appropriations. In comparison, the approval plan for economics appears to be on schedule for the fiscal year.

Using code fields in the funds sometimes enhances flat structures or structures with manually created hierarchies. For instance, the ledger may have only one fund for "Biol" (meaning the biology department), but through the use of codes I can designate each transaction as "Biology" with a code for degree level ("P" = PhD; "M" = Master's; "U" = Undergraduate) and another code for print ("p") or electronic ("e"). A fund transaction coded "Biol, M, e" indicates an electronic resource to support the biology master's program. Figure 8.2 illustrates an order coded to increase granularity in reporting.

Table 8.4 Grouped Fund Information for Approval Hierarchy.

Funds	Pie Chart	Bar Chart	Report		
	Appropriation	Expenditure	Encumbrance	Free Balance	Cash Balance
Approval Economics	$15,000.00	$9,744.81	$110.00	$5,145.19	$5,255.19
Approval English	$15,000.00	$14,748.66	$0.00	$251.34	$251.34
Approval Health	$5,000.00	$2,839.42	$0.00	$2,160.58	$2,160.58
Approval History	$15,000.00	$18,379.78	$0.00	–$3,379.78	–$3,379.78
Approval Math Sci	$5,000.00	$743.09	$1,067.00	$3,189.91	$4,256.91
Approval Literacy	$5,000.00	$3,139.68	$0.00	$1,860.32	$1,860.32
Totals	$60,000.00	$49,595.44	$1,177.00	$9,227.56	$10,404.56

o10122837   Last Updated: 10-26-2011   Created: 03-24-2011   Revisions: 11

Acq Type	p PURCHASE	Est. Price	$1,738.80	Recv Location	s SERIALS
Location	wi Electronic Resources	Form	p PERIODICAL	Billing Location	s SERIALS
Cat Date	- -	Fund	biol Biology	Status	d SERIAL PAD
Claim	- ---	Order Date	03-24-2011	Transit Location	- ---
Copies	1	Order Note	- ---	Vendor	elsvr Elsevier Science
Order Code 1	m MASTERS (2)	Order Type	s SUBSCRIPTION	Language	eng English
Order Code 2	- null	Recv Action	- ---	Country	xxu United States
Order Code 3	- ---	Recv Date	03-31-2011	Volumes	1
Suppress	n SUPPRESS				

Identity   Science Direct Subscribed Titles (perpetual access)
Banner Ref #   10303580

Paid	DATE	INVD	INV#	AMT	VOUCHER	COPIES	FOR CURR	NOTE
	10-26-2011	10-11-2011	M134494	$1,825.74	2078	001		2012: Original adjusted prices incr
Paid	03-31-2011	10-18-2010	M112442	$1,738.80	1214	001		Actual Invoice Price adjusted by 89

Figure 8.2 Order for Biology Subscription.

Notice that the order provides fields to track which degree (master's), which fund (biology), format (print), as well as what type of order (subscription), vendor (Elsevier), and related invoice data. The information provided by these fields allows the acquisition librarian to create reports that delineate which resources support certain programs. For instance, Figure 8.3 shows how the English department appropriation is divided among firm orders, continuations, and print periodicals.

This acquisitions subledger of funds provides the transaction details that support degree programs, grant programs for financial statements, and reporting requirements for other agencies. Creating a well-designed fund structure requires thought and planning up front but provides facile reporting later. An overly elaborate structure decreases flexibility and creates many opportunities for making errors.

Over the years the distinctions in format between book, periodical, microfiche, and video have become less important to track, while the acquisitions of electronic versus print have become more important. At this university, the way these expenditures are tracked has changed. Once, the subledger contained a separate fund for each format. Now, accounting for each format is done simply by designating a format code within the order. Having a flexible ledger structure in the acquisitions module allows the librarian to make changes that

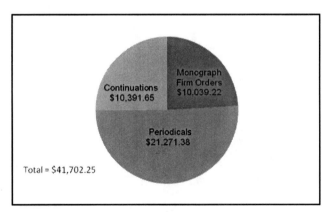

Figure 8.3 English Department Allocation.

support changing reporting needs, while keeping enough consistency in the ledger to make meaningful comparisons in important categories from year to year.

Relationship of Acquisitions Subledger to General Ledger

The acquisitions module acts as a subledger for the library materials account of the general ledger. The general ledger would include an asset account, Library Materials, as well as asset accounts for Buildings and Equipment. The acquisition of library materials that is recorded in the acquisitions module supports and should agree with the cost of library materials added to the Library Materials account in the library's general ledger.

Chapter 9

Internal Controls

An internal control is a process initiated by an organization's board of directors, management, external auditors, or other governing authority designed to provide reasonable assurance of the effectiveness and efficiency of operations, the reliability of financial reporting, and compliance with relevant laws and regulations (Commonwealth of Virginia, Office of the Comptroller 2007, 4). A control is an activity that ensures that the right thing is done at the right time.

A strong internal control framework mitigates risk, which is any event that may have an adverse impact on the library. Examples of risk include, but are not limited to, damage by fire, flood, or theft; stealing or embezzlement; cash flow problems; an untimely death or sickness of key employees; or computer system failures. Internal controls mitigate or reduce the risks of these adverse events.

Maintaining an effective internal control structure depends on more than any one action or circumstance. Four categories of internal control priorities exist. The first category, strategic controls, focuses on high-level goals aligned with the mission of the library. The next category of controls is operations controls. Operation controls emphasize the effectiveness and efficiency of the library within the context of its external environment (business or government). Reporting, the third type of control priority, represents the reliability of reporting, including fulfilling accountability obligations. The fourth type of control is compliance. Compliance requires following applicable laws and regulations and being able to act in accordance with government policy (INTOSAI General Secretariat 2004). This book has focused on reporting so far, but it is important to know the other internal controls.

Eight basic types of control activities comprise internal controls: review and approval; authorization; verification; reconciliation; physical security over assets; segregation of duties; education, training, and coaching; and performance planning and evaluation (Commonwealth of Virginia, Office of the Comptroller 2007, 4). Review and approval procedures are based on the parent organization's policies. Purchases and other financial activities are subject to the review and approval of management. Typically this approval takes the form of a handwritten signature, but it can also be an electronic sign-off through a software package. This signature communicates that the responsible manager has read and approves the financial transaction and how it is being recorded.

Authorization means that the transaction fits within the scope of the parent organization's and the entity's policies. The most obvious example of a transaction that would not be authorized would be an illegal transaction. Another example would be paying wages to an employee who had not provided sufficient identification, such as a driver's license, social security card, or passport. Purchasing an item for the library's collection that was clearly prohibited by the entity's collection development policy could be considered unauthorized. The process of verification proves that the transactions occurred and were correctly recorded, by matching the payment records to the associated check number that cleared the bank account, as well as matching the payment voucher to the vendor's invoice.

Physical security over assets means that books and other materials, equipment and other owned property, are kept safe from theft or damage. Book strips that sound an alarm if a patron attempts to leave the premises without correctly checking out a book through circulation provide physical security. Locks and alarm systems also represent measures to protect the physical security of assets. Having a preservation program is another example of providing physical security.

Segregation of duties refers to the practice of having different individuals responsible for separate steps of processes. If one person is responsible for receiving books and checking off inventory items, while another individual pays for the received items, the chances decrease of paying for items that have not yet been received. One of the reasons is that person in charge of receiving has generated an independent record of receipts that can be externally verified against the vendor's invoice. If an acquisitions librarian or assistant is in charge of the whole process, he or she may feel pressured (because of time demands) to pay an invoice without verifying that each item on the invoice was actually received.

Education, training, and coaching are essential elements of any control structure. Continuing formal education through workshops, seminars, conference attendance, and self-study helps acquisitions librarians and other library employees involved with financial management to cultivate awareness about emerging acquisitions and accounting issues and anticipate how to adapt to these issues.

Training tends to be more skill specific than education. Most vendors provide training (sometimes free) for library staff on their products. All library staff involved in financial management or acquisitions need to receive training in how to use the acquisitions module of the integrated library system (ILS), even if they only view certain screens and run preset reports. In addition, staff need to be trained on the organization's enterprise resource management (ERM) software (PeopleSoft, SAS, Banner, etc.). Your financial library staff should receive 20–30 hours of training per year simply to keep up with the upgrades and changes in the ILS and ERM systems.

Coaching represents another essential element in the internal control framework, because correctly applying the concepts learned in educational and training activities can take a combination of trial and error, practice, and discernment. An individual trying to master these skills will need time, practice, and ongoing feedback.

Performance planning and evaluation promotes intentional reflection by both the librarian and the manager. Opportunities for improvement that have been noted can be addressed with specific training activities in the performance plan. Evaluation of a librarian or library assistant's performance should be a continuation and extension of feedback that occurs throughout the year.

The one part of the internal control framework that we have not yet discussed is performing reconciliations. It will take some dedicated effort to learn and become proficient at reconciling. The following section focuses on performing reconciliations.

Reconciling Transactions between Multiple Information Sources

Reconciliations allow librarians to make sure that the acquisitions information in their ILS agrees with the information that resides in the accounting system of the parent organization. Why is this important? Because the information should be the same in both systems. You are responsible to the parent organization to make sure you have details that support your account balances while you probably track and record your information in the ILS.

In essence, account reconciliation is the process of comparing departmental account records to the reports generated from the financial reporting system of the entity in order to verify the accuracy of each.

Frequently engaging in the reconciliations process forces us to do two things. It forces us to participate in a constant dialogue about how different acquisitions should be classified and recorded. It also helps us monitor account activity and make needed corrections quickly. You may think that the amount of work involved may be prohibitive, but having this level of detail and organization actually saves time spent trying to work backwards to figure out problems.

Transactions processed through the procurement system as well as the accounts payable department are recorded in the account codes for books and periodicals (and/or other categories). The ERM system (Banner, SAS, PeopleSoft) represents the external accounting system, while the ILS acquisitions module represents the library's internal accounting for orders, receipts, returns, and payments for resources. The ERM system includes payments that have already cleared the system in the present year. Transactions in the acquisitions module include resources that have been requested, ordered, received but not yet paid, and paid. Transactions in the acquisitions module appear in the categories designated by the librarians to support reporting; then they are arranged into hierarchies useful for further analysis, with such designations as "PhD Programs" or "College of Business." A public library may want to set up these categories based on program activities, such as "Children's Services" or "Adaptive Technology."

One of the important things an ILS acquisitions module can do that an ERM system cannot always do is to provide a record of resources that have been ordered but not yet paid for through the enterprise-level system.

Collection management compares the paid transactions in these systems to each other during account reconciliation each month and at the end of the year. Collection management reconciles the expenditure information from the acquisitions module's transactions register with transactions that appear in the enterprise-level account codes. This process helps monitor the budget, verify transactions, and identify discrepancies between payments that should have cleared the ERM system and those listed that actually have checks cleared in the system.

An example showing the importance of performing these reconciliations is when in the fall of 2008, one of the central systems units for our organization assigned a cost to our unit via a journal entry of $25,000 that actually belonged to another account (it was a very similar type of transaction to those associated with our account but belonged to another department). The reconciliation process highlighted the $25,000 because it was missing from the acquisitions module's transaction ledger.

How to Reconcile between the Acquisitions Module and ERM System

1. Compare totals for each record type. There will most likely be a difference. Is it big or small?

2. Identify reconciling items.

   a. Reconciling items are often transactions that are treated differently in one system than another. Perhaps one payment was considered paid by the ILS in April but did not make it to the institution's accounts payable department until May1. This transaction would represent a timing difference. These transactions are often considered *payments in transit*.

b. Other typical types of reconciling items include

  (a.) transactions posted to the wrong library account: "Videos" versus "Books" or vice versa.

  (b.) lost-book fees or other fees that are reimbursed directly to the institution's accounting system but bypass the ILS acquisitions module.

  (c.) allocations and journal entries that directly charge expenditures to the institution's accounting system from other branches of the institution or the parent institution.

3. Things to watch for while doing reconciliations (common problems):

  a. Spreadsheet Issues—Make sure the spreadsheet totals are correct (the summation command automatically stops when it reaches an empty cell). Make sure all numbers are correctly formatted as numbers (not as text). Make sure that each record is properly aligned in the correct column (this seems trivial, but it can *really* throw your totals off to have an invoice number in an amount column).

  b. Credits and Credit Memos—These items can get lost in the mix. A vendor may apply a credit memo related to a prior invoice to a recent invoice instead, allowing you to short-pay a current charge. While it may "all come out in the wash" theoretically, in reality you will have payment transactions in the institution's accounting system that are based on the actual cash transactions, but transactions in your acquisitions module that have both the original costs and reductions such as credits associated with the resource.

For example, you pay $200 to a publisher for a one-year subscription to the journal *Library Acquisitions*. Unfortunately, *Library Acquisitions* has a delayed publication schedule, so a couple of months later the publisher credits you $100. The publisher simply applies this credit to your account, and when it reinvoices you for next year's subscription, you receive an invoice for *Library Acquisitions* of $200 less a credit of $100, for a total of $100. The accounting department will see this transaction as a $100 transaction for fiscal year 2012. You will see this as a $200 transaction for this fiscal year's journal subscription and a $100 reduction to last year's journal subscription cost.

Integrated Library System Acquisitions Module

Year 2011:	*Library Acquisitions Journal*	$200
	Less: Credit for journal	–$100
Year 2011	*Library Acquisitions Journal*	$100
Year 2012	*Library Acquisitions Journal*	$200
Institutions Accounting System		
Year 2011:	*Library Acquisitions Journal*	$200
Year 2012	*Library Acquisitions Journal*	$100

Why does this matter? Why not go ahead and track this subscription the same way the accounting department does? Because it will throw off your budget projections for future serials if you base your estimates on the $100 charge. The price of the journal subscription did not decrease. If you base your budget on the lower cost, you will be $100 short the next year.

What Reconciliations Look Like

Table 9.1 illustrates how a reconciliation between the Millennium acquisitions module and our Banner accounts appears at completion.

Final Words on Reconciling Accounts

Performing reconciliations is an art more than a science. You develop a feel for your acquisitions data over time and experience. You will know the stories about each title that you purchase (when, for whom, did you used to get printed copies but now electronic), and that knowledge will help you remember what should be in the accounts and what may be missing. You will develop a stronger sense of what errors are likely to happen and will know where to look without getting lost in the data. As your appreciation of how resources are accounted for grows over time, you will think more strategically about how you evaluate resources and will be able to more easily use techniques such as cost-benefit analysis.

Table 9.1   Reconciliation between Millennium and Banner.

Millennium		Banner		
		Account	Description	Year to Date
Dues and Subscriptions	1,995.00	74000	Operating Expense	-
Firm Orders - Books	169,238.54	74435	Software Maintenance	3,841.56
		74480	Dues and Subscriptions	1,995.00
Approvals - Books	60,257.01	74485	Electronic Media and Database Serv	137,650.33
		74510	Supplies	(872.45)
Standing Order Books - Print	74,329.84	74570	Purchasing Card Supplies	1,232.43
		74580	Electronic Media and Data Bases	-
Standing Order Books - Electronic	132,693.47	78000	Capital Expense Budget Pool	-
		78510	Books	280,202.55
Microfilm - Monographs	1,222.26	78550	Microform	1,336.87
Subtotal	437,741.12		Subtotal	425,386.29
Reconciling Items			Reconciling Items	
Journal Entry for Safari Net books (TBR)	3,146.56		Payments in Transit	11,733.75
MARVCIVE (order type is subscription)	1,575.00			
Ebsco eBook software	225.00			
Microfilm National Book Network, Inc, Invoice 87082	71.57			
GALE Invoice 196941649, should be in Millennium	2,200.00			
Cochrane Library (Included as subscription in Millennium)	3,596.00			
YTD Fees & Feeds	(11,435.21)			
Totals	437,120.04			437,120.04

Section III

Budgeting

Chapter 10

Philosophy of Budgets

t is a plan for allocating resources. Everyone uses budgets in many of their daily lives—for example, time budgets and food budgets to as diets). Allocating resources using a budget plan helps map ways to spend money and other assets to meet personal needs h personal goals. Budgeting and planning go hand in hand, but , planning comes first. You first create the goals and objectives r organization aspires to achieve, and then you decide how you d your resources to accomplish those goals.

at this point that you may notice there is a gap between the necessary to achieve your goals and the actual resources you have . Traditional sources of library funding include local tax support, nty support, state funds (often through grants or project funds to libraries of a library system), federal funds, and the Wisconsin Services and Technology Act (Wisconsin Department of Public on 2008, AE 13), as well as private donations and grants.

ese traditional methods do not bridge the gap, in order to reach als you may need to raise additional funds through more creative ovative techniques. In your quest to identify hidden talents among friends and acquaintances, offer an internship or practicum for grantwriting to a graduate student at a local university or college (with the understanding that the library benefits from the university faculty's established grantwriting capabilities), mine the skills of your volunteers, partner with another organization to share expenses or swap services, or as an

107

absolutely last resort, extend the time frame for achieving your goals. A library must consider many issues when creating a budget.

Unfortunately, many directors and managers have been beaten down by the recent economic situation to a state where they barely and wearily face the upcoming budget process. In this frame of mind, they strive only to cover existing costs (which continue to rise through inflation) with dwindling tax-based revenues when municipal governments instruct agencies to use steady-state budget guidelines. Far too many municipalities have instructed libraries and other agencies to develop budgets using overall reductions guidelines, which call for a certain percentage total decrease in expenditures, or selected reductions guidelines, which target specific decreases such as reduced hours (Wisconsin Department of Public Instruction 2008, AE 13). This perspective is a conservative one, which means just that—the director of the library and the board of directors must fight to conserve the resources and stature of the library and keep it from losing ground (sometimes literally the ground where the building resides). These directors, boards, employees, friends of the library, and other well-wishers have fought to keep the most beneficial programs alive.

While applauding their dedication, try to distance yourself (as a director or budget manager) from too beleaguered a mindset while creating a budget. Try to remain neutral (neither overly optimistic nor pessimistic), and keep both your long- and short-range goals as well as your utmost dreams for the library in the front of your mind during the process. Try to instill this attitude in your board or respective funding source by continuing to focus on what *can* be achieved and what those accomplishments can mean to the wider community that your library serves. Otherwise, your library will be buffeted around from one year's budget crisis to the next, trying to find shelter wherever you can, but lacking any real sense of direction.

So, the first point to keep in mind is that the budget derives from the goals. The budget should not create the goals or construct the limits for those goals. Avoid budgeting philosophies that ask you to concentrate on the fixed costs first and postpone goal setting until the budget planners determine whether there may be any money left lying around afterwards.

The second point is that we need to take a brief detour from budgeting to the topic of long-term and short-term goals. The leadership and the engaged community of your library should share five to ten ambitious goals to be realized within 5 years, as well as two or three goals to be realized in 6, 12, and 18 months. These goals should be stated publically and reaffirmed frequently. These goals will drive the budget process.

The Library of Congress is an excellent example of a library that publishes its strategic plan in its annual report along with its financial statements and budgetary reports (Library of Congress 2011, 1). Although it is not surprising to see the Library of Congress taking leadership by creating a strategic plan that directs its budgeting, financial, operations, and activities, this example remains instructive. In the following quote from its 2010 report, the Library of Congress adeptly connects its strategic plan to its budget on:

The strategic plan's goals not only set broad outcomes that each of the ten major organizations relate to, but also establish broad strategies to be followed and define performance indicators to determine progress toward achieving the goals and outcomes. Supported by a rigorous annual program performance planning process, and regular program performance assessment reviews, the strategic plan ensures Library organizations are all working toward common ends and provides the background guidance for the Library's annual Congressional Budget Justification requests. (Library of Congress 2011, 1)

The budgeting process occurs once a year. Once you establish your organization's budget, it faces the process of gaining approval from your community (municipalities—school systems, state, and county governments), your parent organization (for-profit organizations, state organizations, nonstate or nongovernment nonprofits), or your federal agency.

During the budget approval process, your funding source may say that it cannot provide all of the funds that you require. Be prepared for this contingency—it is likely during this economic situation. It was always likely during my professional career, which began quite a few years before the current economic situation. Realize that you and your library budget are walking into the world of "No." Be prepared to fight "Yes." A high probability exists that some alderman, elected official, or other member of the public will try to gently or not-so-gently explain to you the "facts" along the lines of . . .

These are hard times. There just isn't enough money to go around. I care just as much about puppet shows/story times/adult literacy/information literacy/health informatics as the next [completely-out-of-touch-politician-who-is-probably-a-college-drop-out] person. What this county/city/country needs first and foremost is job creation. And that means cutting taxes . . . And that means cutting library support. (Hypothetical Library Nonsupporter)

Stay calm, focused, and deliver your well-prepared response along the lines of the following rebuttal:

Your well-intended concern about using tax revenue to support the library is one that is well understood. Four responses cover this situation: (1) Public libraries such as yours represent a wise investment of tax dollars that yield a quantifiable return on this investment for the community; (2) The citizens of our community deserve access to high-quality, timely, and relevant information; (3) The cost of not providing library services is prohibitive and would decimate the quality of life for the entire community; and (4) Small businesses use the public library to survive and thrive.

Have a presentation ready that includes the following support or something similar.

(1) *Libraries give a good return on investment of tax dollars.*
   The Saint Louis Public Library conducted a research study and concluded "that each $1 of annual tax support for the library produces, on average, direct benefits to users of more than $4."[1]

(2) *Citizens deserve access.*

Providing information services for our working families, our retired seniors, and our veterans is extending a public service that has been earned by our citizens through their service and their taxes. These information services connect our community members to health information that helps them to be an active and informed citizenry empowered to take care of their health. The result of this empowerment is the reduction of health care costs for themselves and our community. The early literacy services that the library provides through story time, summer reading, and after-school programs establishes a level of readiness for K–12 education that gives students an advantage lasting through 3rd grade; also, for those reading-ready students, it reduces the necessity of other paid staff.

(3) *The cost of not providing library services is prohibitive.*

The Saint Louis Public Library study estimated that the value the library brings to the community by leveraging combined resources far exceeds what individuals could accomplish separately without the library.[2] While the library in this study is on a different scale than our library, we provide these same services [list similar services].

(4) *Small businesses use the library to survive and thrive.*

[If possible, provide pictures and testimonies of business owners from your community.]In the United States, small business owners use resources at public libraries at an average rate of 2.8 million times every month (OCLC 2010).

The sources cited above provide information for the unbelieving, the unwilling to believe, and the unwilling to pay. Should you find yourself in a less hostile budget climate, tailor your budget presentation to highlight the history of benefits that your organization has continued to provide for your community, illustrating many specific examples, quantifying services, and including many pictures. The State Library of Iowa's library services provide a resource called *For Libraries—Telling the Library Story*, which provides templates and scripts for budget presentations, including suggested props and a sample photo consent form.

Another highly recommended source is *Opportunity for All: How the American Public Benefits from Internet Access at U.S. Libraries* (Becker et al. 2010). This report provides many helpful statistics, such as libraries' impact on communities' educational, entrepreneurial, health, and financial activities.

In conclusion, do not lose hope. Your efforts are amplifying throughout the country even though you may not be able to hear them or see the results immediately. You will.

Now that you have done the necessary mindful preparation, it is time to talk about application.

Notes

1. This calculation considers past public investments in buildings and collections. Current users are reaping returns not only from current public funds supporting the library, but also from the foresight and generosity of past tax and philanthropic support. "Yet, no matter how generous or lavish the past investment, it is current tax support that permits users to access collections conveniently, receive staff assistance to find and use collections effectively, and assure that the collections built up over time through past investment will continue to be preserved" (Holt, Elliott, and Moore 1999; http://www.slpl.lib.mo.us/libsrc/resresul.htm; accessed 1/19/2012).

2. The researchers in the Saint Louis Public Library study identified every service they provided and assigned conservative market values based on comparative providers. The financial equivalent amount of resources made available to the Saint Louis community was $157.5 million (Holt, Elliott, and Moore 1999; http://www.slpl.lib.mo.us/libsrc/resresul.htm; accessed 1/19/2011).

Chapter 11

Practicalities of Budgets

The next topic is how do librarians budget for their libraries? Municipal and state libraries covered by the Governmental Accounting Standards Board (GASB) can look to that body for direction on this issue. Statement No. 34, paragraphs 130 (as amended by Statement No. 41) and 131 say that you should have an annual budget, monitor it, and compare the budget with actual expenditures in a way that makes it possible to identify any instances of spending in excess of the legally adopted budget (Kinnersley and Patton 2005). The standards say that the entity should have an annual budget that is approved through a public budget process, and the budget must be compared to actual expenditures. Because the budget's audience includes the library board, mayor, the municipal or state government finance committee, the state or municipal government, the members of the public who attend the budget hearing, and, ultimately, the general public, a well-constructed budget should have these characteristics:

1. Clarity: The budget presentation should be clear enough so every board member, every employee, and every municipal governing body member can understand what is being represented.

2. Accuracy: Budget documentation must support the validity of budget figures, and figures must be transcribed and reported carefully without variation from the documentation.

3. Consistency: Budget presentation should retain the same format from period to period so that comparisons can be easily made.

All budgets are comparative devices, used to show how what is being done now compares with what happened in the past and what is projected to happen in the future.

4. Comprehensiveness: Budget reports should include as complete a picture of fiscal activities as possible. The only way to know the true cost of the library operation is to be certain that all revenue and expenditure categories are included within the budget. (Wisconsin Department of Public Instruction 2008)

A typical budget calendar includes several stages. Many of these stages depend on the initiative and competency of the library director. The first stage, the preparation stage, occurs early in the fiscal year, soon after publishing the prior year's annual report. In the preparation stage, the director reviews the annual report, as well as other available financial and nonquantitative data and analysis, in order to identify trends and patterns as well as begin matching library resources to services and activities (Michigan Department of Education 2002; Wisconsin Department of Public Instruction 2008).

In the second stage, the director shares the trend analysis with the library board, who has already received copies of the prior year's annual report as well as additional analysis. The third stage occurs in the middle of the fiscal year and involves both the director and the board. The director and the board review expenditures and revenues of the current budget as well as budget guidelines. The board discusses and provides the director with guidelines to create the new budget. While these activities are happening at the library, the municipal or state government has generally begun establishing the budget calendar and guidelines. During the fourth stage, the director drafts the preliminary budget and budget presentation for the board. The fifth stage consists of the board's initial review of the preliminary budget, their revision or approval, and the director's resulting adjustments and resubmission to the board. If the board approves the resubmitted budget, the director submits the budget to the appropriate government body (Wisconsin Department of Public Instruction 2008, 1–2). This stage is usually completed by late summer or early fall.

During the fall, the sixth stage, or "adoption" stage, occurs. The mayor, finance committee, or other relevant government administrator reviews the library budget and, if necessary, requests additional information from either the library director or library board. Within the adoption stage, the legislative body, such as a municipality, holds a budget hearing and officially reviews and potentially amends the budget. Budget hearings are open to the public, and members of the public may comment on the library budget before it is approved. The last stage, execution, is the year-end appropriation or adjustment of expenditures prior to government appropriation. In this stage, budgetary accounts are set up to record the estimated revenues and expenditures for appropriate funds (Michigan Department of Education 2002; Wisconsin Department of Public Instruction 2008, 1–2).

Budgeting Technique

Good budgeting techniques include developing effective estimates, monitoring expenses against the budget, and controlling costs. Effective budget monitoring depends on a well-structured and well-maintained accounting system.

Beginning the Budget Process

Budgeting for Specific Goals (Done First!)

For the purposes of first year, consider the goals to be realized in 6, 12, and 18 months as separate projects according to your strategic plan. Create a list of all equipment, personnel, and external expenses (advertising, contracted skilled labor, additional supplies, transportation, etc.) that will be needed to accomplish the goals. Get quotes and estimates, ask for volunteers from your friends groups, and begin to use informal networks to see who has what kinds of skills that they may be willing to volunteer.

Budget Fixed Costs

Fixed costs are those costs which the library would still have to pay under almost any condition, including even if not a single patron walked through the door for the next month and no hourly paid employees came to work. The library would have to pay rent (or mortgage), electricity, water, and other utilities, insurance, salaries of exempt employees, and benefits of all full-time employees.

For most individuals the concept of fixed costs is intuitive, because so many fixed costs exist in our personal lives and households. Many of them are the same as those the library incurs, such as rent/mortgage, utilities, and insurance. Some are slightly different, like salaries and benefits. All of them, just like the costs for individuals, are always increasing. Utility and insurance rates increase. Salaries and the costs of benefits (such as health insurance) also continue to rise.

The budget is built on estimates. Knowing exact information about the future will always remain beyond your grasp. Generally, your organization should have a schedule for lease or mortgage payments, but the increases in other costs are difficult to anticipate. Become comfortable with reasoned and researched educated estimates. Fixed costs can be deceivingly difficult to budget, despite the category's name of "fixed." What the term *fixed costs* really means is that "We will always have to pay insurance, but we don't know how much it is going to be next year." The budgeting process strives to makes realistic estimates of these fixed costs, based on reasonable calculations from both the history of the cost and what can be known about the way it increases from year to year.

For determining utilities, insurance, security system costs, landscaping charges, and other expenditures associated with maintenance of the building, the prior year's cost can be adjusted for an inflation rate that has been published or calculated by taking an average of the last five (or three) year-to-year increases.

The highest percentage of many libraries' budget is the cost of salaries, wages, and associated benefits. This information may come as a surprise to many library employees.

If you are in the process of hiring a new employee, but the salary or benefits (or person) has not been determined yet, use an estimate for the budget. If your library or parent organization has a human resources office, they can assist you in developing a reasonable estimate. If you are a library director of a small library who does not have access to a human resources specialist, find an average published salary for a librarian or library staff member (via the American Library Association's Web site, www.ala.org), or for other professions through professional sites on the Internet or the *Occupational Outlook Handbook* (U.S. Bureau of Labor Statistics 2011), or average salaries of occupations in your area through a local employment center.

After you identify an average base salary, compute an estimate for benefits. If you have another recently hired employee, it should be relatively painless to determine what percentage of that employee's total compensation is comprised of nonsalary benefits by consulting the payroll. If a current employee has a salary of $35,000 and a total compensation package of $50,000 (including vacation days, sick days, insurance), then the salary will be 70% of the entire estimated compensation. If you plan to hire an individual at an annual salary of $50,000, budget $71,500 as the position's total compensation.

Budget Variable Costs

Variable costs fluctuate based on activity. If there is a children's program where local daycare facilities bring toddlers to the local public library for story times and crafts, and it explodes because of a wildly popular duo of talented librarians (I'm talking about you, Abingdon, Virginia, but certainly not only you), then many related costs will begin to shoot up. The cost of toilet paper and pipe cleaners needed to create all those special flowers, the cost of toilet paper unrelated to craft flowers, increased hourly personnel costs, the increased costs of snacks provided, etc., will all rise precipitously. In nonprofit organizations, successful programs do not sustain themselves by increased profits; there are no profits.

In some nonprofit/ government organizations, there are some cost recovery mechanisms. Examples include utilities such as water and electricity, where you are charged a fee based on your usage to cover the cost to the municipality of making those services available to you. There are no cost recovery programs for a story time for three-year-olds. It is not feasible to institute a $3.00 cover charge at the library for preschoolers, although it would still be a bargain in terms of the value exchanged. As a program aimed at early literacy succeeds, it uses more resources—resources like the (labor) time of the librarian and staff who select the resources; plan the programming; pre-prepare the crafts; select and practice the songs, finger-puppets, and puppet plays; plan and orchestrate the games so that everyone (including the physically handicapped and developmentally delayed) engages in the activity; choose the theme of each program and the associated storybooks; and deliver the performance (which truly must be a performance to successfully capture and sustain the attention of 20 to 25 preschool children for 15 to 20 minutes for storybooks, even including breaks for songs and finger plays).

In addition to the demand for more program sessions by these librarians as their fame spreads, children actually want to go to the library and want to take books home with them. This phenomenon leads to more demands on staffing and increased acquisition of books. The nature of this phenomenon is the basis of the term *variable costs*. In the nonprofit world, an increase in variable costs is often the result of successful programming, excellent librarians, talented staff, and effective marketing. Ironically, this success requires more funds, potentially funds beyond what may have been originally budgeted, and, as a result, the director of the library may incur criticism for not managing to the bottom line effectively. Being able to both illustrate in human terms and quantify in economic terms the rewards of children's reading readiness as they enter the public school system can mitigate people's concerns regarding a library's increased variable costs.

Another option to employ when describing increased variable costs, which by their nature display the success of a specific program, is to talk about them in terms of being *an investment in the future of our community*. Emphasize that this investment is not an ethereal platitude but a social contract between citizens—benefactor and receiver, adult and child— to preserve and build upon the foundations of the current community. While the children of the most affluent citizens of a small town may move away as adults for better career options, the adult children that remain foster their community identities, their relationships and their children's relationships with those institutions that they have grown to trust. These relationships are reinforced through family and community programming held at the public library, genealogy workshops, and summer reading programs. Long-time citizens of the community who have participated in these programs or whose family members have been enriched by them provide an excellent donor base for fundraising, as well as a potentially intricately bound and interrelated broad web of political support when a public library budget has to be approved as part of the municipal process.

Budgeting for Materials

The next major part of variable costs is the acquisitions or materials budget. Other than salaries and wages (labor), the materials budget may be the largest part of the entire budget. In addition, in recent years the costs of books, periodicals, and databases have increased beyond the rate of inflation.

As is the situation with most libraries, our library's electronic resources continue to cannibalize a growing percentage of the budget. Around one-half of the Ebsco titles are electronic (approximately $500,000). Elsevier titles are close to $500,000, and other electronic journal packages (Wiley, $106,000; Emerald, $87,000; Ebrary, $54,000; Westlaw, $40,000; Sage, $50,000; Oxford, $40,000) reach approximately $375,000; this brings us to a total of $1,377,000 for major electronic resource packages out of an overall combined $2.7million-dollar materials budget. Electronic journals are budgeted differently from other electronic resources; journals are budgeted based on historical price increases. Each journal resource is budgeted as though the expectation is that the library will continue to renew it for the next five years, and the current rate of increase will persist. Budgeting at the individual resource level provides perspective about what the budget can or cannot absorb when considering new resources.

In a quest to find "the right way," or at least a better way, Dr. G. Robert Smith Jr., a noted authority in governmental and nonprofit accounting and reporting, was interviewed (G. R. Smith Jr., personal communication, 2009, 2012). Dr. Smith is an associate professor at Middle Tennessee State University and the American Accounting Association's representative on the Governmental Accounting Standards Advisory Council (GASAC). This body "is responsible for consulting with the GASB on technical issues on the Board's agenda, project priorities, matters likely to require the attention of the GASB, selection and organization of task forces, and such other matters as may be requested by the GASB or its chairman" (GASAC, http://www.gasb.org/jsp/GASB/Page/GASBSectionPage&cid =1176156726962, 2012).

Dr. Smith discussed how to best to budget for library acquisitions in a way that includes inflationary factors. It was my objective to create a model for materials budget that would include various hypothetical situations that could be applied to many different libraries. Dr. Smith was very convincing in his suggestion that it would be more powerful to present our actual commitments, adjusted for inflation, against projected flat budget funding from the university. The materials budget provides a blueprint of the acquisitions activities for the fiscal year; it proceeds through monthly or quarterly assessments and reconciliations, finally arriving at the day-to-day practices that support the "big picture."

This budget forecast, shown in Table 11.1, needs to be interpreted in light of several factors. The first factor was the application of an average inflation rate based on increases from the prior year. For print periodicals, the inflation factor was budgeted based on last year's inflation. The second consideration was to keep budgeted funds the same for each year based on a flat budget estimate (which is very realistic, if not optimistic for some libraries). The third issue is to account for hosting fees for one-time purchases as continuations. GASB Statement No. 34 allows you to capitalize costs associated with making a resource available for use.

While everyone is aware that inflation consumes a larger and larger portion of each year's budget, it is difficult to appreciate the cumulative effect of inflation each year without looking at the calculation. For the purposes of this calculation, assume that all materials are being renewed for five years at constant interest rates. For each resource, the previous year's cost is multiplied by 1 + the inflation factor for that resource. For instance, the library paid

Table 11.1 Periodicals Budget Forecast.

Base Budget	Inflation Factor	Year One Year Ending 2011	Year Two Year Ending 2012	Year Three Year Ending 2013	Year Four Year Ending 2014	Year Five Year Ending 2015
Periodical Payments						
Ebsco Renewal Invoice		$ 1,174,538.00	$ 1,350,718.70	$ 1,593,848.07	$ 1,880,740.72	$ 2,219,274.05
Directs						
American Chemical Society	5.00%	$ 53,125.00	$ 55,781.25	$ 58,570.31	$ 61,498.83	$ 64,573.77
Berkeley Electronic Press	8.00%	$ 1,938.00	$ 2,093.04	$ 2,260.48	$ 2,441.32	$ 2,636.63
Blackwell/John Wiley	8.00%	$ 104,915.00	$ 113,308.20	$ 122,372.86	$ 132,162.68	$ 142,735.70
Cerebral Cortex	5.00%	$ -	$ -	$ -		
Chronicle of Higher Education	5.00%	$ 5,661.00	$ 5,944.05	$ 6,241.25	$ 6,553.32	$ 6,880.98
Duke Periodicals - direct	5.00%	$ 4,850.45	$ 5,141.48	$ 5,449.97	$ 5,776.96	$ 6,123.58
Elsevier (Base + Freedom Coll)	5.00%	$ 550,055.40	$ 577,558.17	$ 606,436.08	$ 636,757.88	$ 668,595.78
Emerald	5.00%	$ 87,212.00	$ 92,444.72	$ 97,991.40	$ 103,870.89	$ 110,103.14
JAMA	8.00%	$ 3,000.00	$ 3,300.00	$ 3,630.00	$ 3,993.00	$ 4,392.30
NAPC & Proquest Microform	8.00%	$ 18,253.85	$ 20,079.24	$ 22,087.16	$ 24,295.87	$ 26,725.46
Miscellaneous Direct Periodicals	8.00%	$ 10,246.04	$ 11,270.64	$ 12,397.71	$ 13,637.48	$ 15,001.22
MIT COGNET	10.00%	$ 2,491.00	$ 2,889.56	$ 3,351.89	$ 3,888.19	$ 4,510.30
National Bureau of Econ Research	5.00%	$ 775.00	$ 813.75	$ 854.44	$ 897.16	$ 942.02
Nature	10.00%	$ 12,325.00	$ 13,557.50	$ 14,913.25	$ 16,404.58	$ 18,045.03
Oxford 2008	7.00%	$ 34,216.64	$ 36,611.80	$ 39,174.63	$ 41,916.86	$ 44,851.04
Proquest/CSA (Culture Grams)	5.00%	$ 2,491.00	$ 2,615.55	$ 2,746.33	$ 2,883.64	$ 3,027.83
Sage	8.00%	$ 56,196.11	$ 59,005.92	$ 61,956.21	$ 65,054.02	$ 68,306.72
Science	10.00%	$ 7,545.00	$ 8,299.50	$ 9,129.45	$ 10,042.40	$ 11,046.63
Serials Solutions Marc Records	10.00%	$ 18,145.00	$ 19,959.50	$ 21,955.45	$ 24,151.00	$ 26,566.09
SPARC	5.00%	$ 5,600.00	$ 5,880.00	$ 6,174.00	$ 6,482.70	$ 6,806.84
Total Estimated Periodical Costs		$ 2,153,579.49	$ 2,387,272.56	$ 2,691,540.93	$ 3,043,449.49	$ 3,451,145.11
Flat Budget for Periodicals		$ 2,233,504.00	$ 2,233,504.00	$ 2,233,504.00	$ 2,233,504.00	$ 2,233,504.00
Surplus/Shortfall		$ 79,924.51	$ (153,768.56)	$ (458,036.93)	$ (809,945.49)	$ (1,217,641.11)

$12,325 for the publication *Nature* in the first year, 2011. Given the budget formula, the estimate for 2012 would be $12,325 * 1.10 = $13,557.50. The estimate for 2013 would be $13,557.50 * 1.10, or $14,913.25.

In the Surplus/Shortfall line at the bottom of the table, the effect of inflation on flat budgets over a five-year period becomes clearer. As you can see, over the five years about one-fourth to one-third of your library's purchasing power disappears due to inflation if your materials budget is not adjusted upwards to cover it. While you may need to tweak this example for your own institution, this could be a powerful visual aid in explaining to funding sources the need for materials budget increases.

Monitoring the Budget

Comparing budgeted costs with actual expenditures should occur at least quarterly and at most monthly. In the budget categories, discrepancies between the expected and actual expenditures should be identified and explained. In addition, the person in charge of monitoring the budget should use an appropriate rationale to indicate whether the differences between specific budgeted and actual expenditures will continue at the same rate throughout the year, increase, or reverse. If costs in a particular budget category appear to continue to increase in excess of the budget, an adjustment may need to be made. The expected difference will need to be subtracted from another budget category in order to balance the budget. In the section of this chapter that deals with controlling costs, we will return to the idea of making adjustments and explore various options for addressing budget excesses.

Differences between budgeted and actual expenditures that simply do not make sense need to be researched. Expenditures should be verified by checking them against external sources, such as cancelled checks or copies of paid invoices from vendors.

Using Budgets to Help Control Costs

Three techniques that can control costs are selective cancellation of ongoing materials, negotiation, and cost-benefit analysis. Cancellation is such a dirty word, isn't it? It evokes images of angry faculty members protesting the library's actions, nasty editorials in the local newspaper, as well as actually processing the cancellations from an acquisitions point of view. One method of cancellation is to send lists of periodical titles to departments and ask them to rank the periodicals in order of importance. Another variation is to ask the department to cut a certain dollar amount from the list of titles that are purchased on behalf of that department. Neither of these methods is very popular with teaching faculty or with librarians.

As difficult as it is, periodical cancellation is a necessary, if unpleasant, ongoing responsibility of librarians to ensure that the periodicals stay relevant for the university's changing needs. With the current costs of periodicals, many organizations simply cannot afford to keep collecting titles that are not being used.

Here is one strategy that may help lessen the pain. It is not a perfect plan, and you will be able to spot the flaws. They will be addressed in order. Create a limited cancellation list. Decide certain parameters that would make it easy to target expensive, rarely used materials. Our parameters were 1) the title was accessed electronically less than 25 times in the past 12-month period and 2) the title costs at least $200.00 per year. The serials librarian ran the usage statistics. At the beginning, the list held around 300 titles that in total represented close to $240,000. Faculty representatives were asked to share these lists with their colleagues and ask how they felt about cancelling them. Even if you do not ultimately have to carry out such a plan because a variety of factors (including stimulus funds) saves you, starting to discuss this possibility with your faculty representatives gains their support. Faculty members understand that it is difficult to pay for expensive materials that are not being used.

Words of Caution

You may have some objections to this process. Know that the author agrees with most of them. Just because a journal is rarely used in one 12-month period does not mean that it will not be used heavily in the next year. Just because a journal is rarely used in one year does not mean that it has not been highly used in the last three years. Many unused titles may possibly be omitted from consideration because they do not meet the $200.00 threshold. Yes, that is true. However, if you are short on staff, it is less labor intensive to cancel one $1,000 title than it is cancel 20 titles that cost $50 each. It might be difficult to consider print titles because you may have no way of measuring their usage. You can cancel online periodicals based on 25 or fewer uses. An unfair standard? Yes, it is. Especially since most librarians know that usage of their print periodicals has dropped significantly.

Otto von Bismarck once remarked that "politics is considered the art of the possible" (August 11, 1867)—an effective periodical cancellation is an art of the feasible. As you eventually convert your print titles to online, you will track their usage as well and perhaps cancel when appropriate. This periodical cancellation strategy is offered as an alternative to the more painful and drawn out practices that include all titles, all departments, and sometimes all faculty members. It also has one more advantage. Because you are dealing with a less exhaustive list of titles, it is possible to allow all faculty members to see all 300 titles up for elimination. Faculty members become aware of title cancellations outside their own discipline. In addition, the faculty has opportunity to alert the library when important interdisciplinary titles are up for cancellation. Using this method librarians can plan to keep titles where the cancellation is contested based on current curricular or scholarly needs.

Negotiation as a Technique to Reduce Budgeted Costs

Resource procurement begins with negotiation. At the end of April, vendors are contacted about items on the wish list. Generally, the vendors are asked about several things: whether they are able to give any end-of-year price breaks, how their pricing structures work, if their models are built on perpetual access, what are the long-term costs such as hosting fees, if caps exists for the hosting fees, whether there are limitations on access, whether there are interlibrary loan possibilities, and/or other considerations.

There are often some ways to negotiate in order to save money. The library might agree to longer contract terms to limit the inflation factor. Other possibilities include keeping the electronic resource but subscribing to fewer seat licenses. Another possibility is going from a site license to individual seat licenses.

The other type of negotiation that the acquisitions librarian performs is renewal negotiation, in which the publisher offers an incentive to transition from print resources to electronic resources. In these cases, the original format of the content was a monograph, microform series, or monographic series, and one publisher owns all of the content. The acquisitions librarian individually negotiates the contracts based on feedback from faculty associated with the department fund. Price can be negotiated based on seat licenses. These negotiations are ongoing throughout the year.

Sometimes negotiating requires performing cost-benefit analysis of the resource compared to a similar resource. Performing cost-benefit analysis provides a good platform for negotiating with vendors because, as the library director or acquisitions librarian, you can argue why certain features are more important to your constituents than features that the vendor is offering. You can ask that the price be adjusted to reflect the disadvantage. Are you familiar with cost-benefit analysis?

> Cost-Benefit Analysis is an analytical technique that compares the social costs and benefits of proposed programs or policy actions. All losses and gains experienced by society are included and measured in dollar terms. The net benefits created by an action are calculated by subtracting the losses incurred by some sectors of society from the gains that accrue to others. Alternative actions are compared to choose one or more that yield the greatest net benefits, or ratio of benefits to costs. The inclusion of all gains and losses to society in cost-benefit analysis distinguishes it from cost-effectiveness analysis, which is a more limited view of costs and benefits. (Michigan State Budget Office, Department of Technology, Management and Budget)

Comparison of similar resources requires estimating the benefits to the users or constituents as well as delineating the costs over the estimated useful life (in this case, the life of the contract). Benefits to users might include number of titles, subject coverage, ability to cooperate with existing library technology, ease of access for remote users, technical support, perpetual access, availability of training, and intuitive interface design. More categories of benefits exist than are listed here. When generating categories for comparison, make sure to list all attributes that you consider essential in your mission to provide access to these sources and meet the specific needs of the faculty, staff, and students that require them.

Costs include direct costs, such as the price of the subscription or purchased content and access fees. Indirect costs include factors such as the time electronic resource librarians spend integrating the resource into the library's catalog, federated search program, and an A-to-Z list or Serials Solutions product; time associated with obtaining technical support; as well as time training or retraining reference and instruction librarians. Consider also the cost of time needed to prepare all of the purchase requisitions, contracts, and related paperwork necessary to sign a contract at your institution. Good technical support and easy integration of a resource into the library's electronic collection saves valuable and scarce time that can be used to further the library's mission more effectively. This savings of time should be estimated in terms of money to assist in clarifying the decisions.

An example of cost-benefit analysis in comparing two similar resources is included in Table 11.2.

The direct costs are the easiest to enumerate. The more difficult challenge is to quantify your indirect costs. Do not be afraid to make educated estimates. Ask the people who work most closely with the product to give their best approximation for how long it takes them to support the product. Let them think about it long enough to let all kinds of specific memories come back to them so they can come up with a realistic estimate. Remember, there are

Table 11.2 Cost-Benefit Analysis of Two Databases.

Cost-Benefit Analysis of Two Databases	Database A	Database B
Annual Subscription	$ 40,000.00	$ 60,000.00
Number of titles	200	325
Cost per title	$ 200.00	$ 184.62
Number of Disciplines Served		
Mass Comm, Recording Industry, Elec Media, Journalism	4	
Mass Comm, Broadcast Journalism, Elec Media, Advertising		5
Pubic Relations		
Number of Graduate Programs Served	3	3
Ease of Access		
Reputation	Good	Fair
Technical Support	Fair	Unknown
Internal Maintenance (Estimated in hours annually)	20	30
Maintenance expressed in librarian salary	$ 600.00	$ 900.00
Integrates with Federated Search?	Yes	Yes
Usage		
Prior year full-text views	6000	N/A
Cost per usage	$ 6.67	X
How much usage would it take for Database B to compare favorably to Database A?		
Divide $60,000 by 6.66		9009
Contract Issues		
Hours spent annually on licensing and contracts		
Addendum only	4	
All new forms		20
Multiply librarian's annual rate to get estimated cost	$ 120.00	$ 600.00

no perfect estimates. Talking through the issues that are included in the estimate allows for a more robust consideration of the alternatives and may spur colleagues to remember other important factors for consideration. Title counts are relatively easily done through Serials Solutions' overlap analysis or Microsoft Access's de-duplication query.

Cost-benefit analysis allows librarians to go back to the negotiating table with valuable feedback for vendors. In addition, librarians are better prepared to negotiate about features that are most important to the services they deliver and those that they would be willing to give up for a lower price. Providing a rationale for why a specific resource better meets your needs gives vendors a chance to tailor their products or tailor their pricing options. What tends to happen in situations where you do not use a thorough cost-benefit approach is that you and other librarians become intoxicated with the interesting possibilities of all the new features. Many times those features, no matter how interesting and impressive, do not address the current and manifest needs of your faculty and students. Sometimes you may even spend time that you cannot afford promoting these new features and integrating them into instruction courses. If you stand back and try to quantify the hours spent promoting, training, and instructing, you can appreciate that the process is expensive and maybe too expensive given your staffing.

Afterword

Hopefully this book will encourage acquisitions librarians and other librarians responsible for financial management to feel more confident in their abilities. While this book explored many acquisitions and financial management topics, its main purpose was to introduce and make accessible basic accounting concepts, as well as to direct librarians to resources that will enhance their skills. Financial statements from some of the most financially sophisticated and respected libraries in the United States were used as examples to illustrate the complexity of these issues. At the same time, it was necessary to keep the issues down to earth enough that librarians in smaller libraries can apply these principles.

Please advance your knowledge by reviewing the sources listed in the References section as well as researching applicable accounting policies and procedures for your state. It is also important that you use your position as an acquisitions or financial management librarian to promote education and training in these areas for others.

References

American Library Association. (1996). *Library Bill of Rights*. Retrieved from ALA.org http://www.ala.org/advocacy/intfreedom/librarybill.

American Library Association. (2012). ALA JobList. Retrieved from http://joblist.ala.org/.

Barstow, S. (2002). "One Librarian's Journey: A Transition from Department Head to Assistant Director." *Bottom Line: Managing Library Finances* 15 (15). Retrieved from http://www.emeraldinsight.com/journals.htm?issn=0888-045X&volume=15&issue=1&articleid=1486351&show=html.

Becker, S., M. D. Crandall, K. E. Fisher, B. Kinney, C. Landry, and A. Rocha. (2010). *Opportunity for All: How the American Public Benefits from Internet Access at U.S. Libraries*. Washington, DC: U.S. Government Printing Office.

California Department of Finance. (2005). *Budgeting and Accounting Relationship*. Retrieved from California Department of Finance: http://www.dof.ca.gov/fisa/bag/relation.htm.

Capella Education Company. (2011). *Annual Report Pursuant to Section 13 or 15(d) of the Securities Exchange Act of 1934, for the Fiscal Year Ended December 31, 2010* (Commission File Number: 001-33140). Retrieved from U.S. Securities and Exchange Commission: http://www.sec.gov/Archives/edgar/data/1104349/000119312511047299/d10k.htm.

Carr, D. (1970). "Husserl's Problematic Concept of the Life-World." *American Philosophical Quarterly* 7 (4): 331–339.

Commonwealth of Virginia, Office of the Comptroller. (2007). *Function No. 20900—Reconciliation Procedures* (Topic No. 20905—CARS Reconciliation Requirements). Retrieved from Virginia Department of Accounts: http://www.doa.virginia.gov/Admin_Services/CAPP/CAPP_Topics/20905.pdf.

Dearstyne, B. W. (2010). "Management of Information Programs and Services, INFM 612 Course Syllabus" [Syllabus]. Retrieved from University of Maryland, Management of Information Programs and Services: http://ischool.umd.edu/pdf/courses/2010/INFM%20612%20Dearstyne%20Spring%202010.pdf.

Federal Accounting Standards Advisory Board. (2011). *FASAB Handbook*, Version 10. Retrieved from http://www.fasab.gov/pdffiles/2011_fasab_handbook.pdf.

Federal Library and Information Center Committee. (2004). *Handbook of Federal Librarianship* [White Paper]. Retrieved from Library of Congress, Federal Library and Information Center Committee: http://www.loc.gov/flicc.

Financial Accounting Standards Board. (1993). *Financial Statements of Not-for-Profit Organizations* (FAS No. 117). Norwalk, CT: Financial Accounting Standards Board.

Financial Accounting Standards Board. (2010). *Statement of Financial Accounting Concepts* (No. 8). Retrieved from FASB.org: http://www.fasb.org/home.

Fisher, W. (2001). "Core Competencies for the Acquisitions Librarian." *Library Collections, Acquisitions, & Technical Services* 25:179–190.

Governmental Accounting Standards Board. (n.d.). Governmental Accounting Standards Advisory Council. Retrieved from http://www.gasb.org/jsp/GASB/Page/GASBSectionPage&cid=1176156726962.

Governmental Accounting Standards Board. (2006). *GASB White Paper: Why Governmental Accounting and Financial Reporting Is—and Should Be—Different*. Retrieved from GASB.org: www.gasb.org/home.

Holt, G. E., D. Elliott, and A. Moore. (1999). "Placing a Value on Public Libraries." *St. Louis Public Library Premier Library Sources*. Retrieved from St. Louis Public Library January 19, 2012: http://www.slpl.lib.mo.us/libsrc/resresul.htm.

Indianapolis-Marion County Public Library. (2011). *Comprehensive Annual Financial Report for the Year Ending December 31, 2010*. Retrieved from Indianapolis-Marion County Public Library: http://www.imcpl.org/files/1913/3242/0665/imcpl2010cafr.pdf.

Institute of Museum and Library Services. (2011). *Public Libraries in the United States: Fiscal Year 2009* (IMLS-2011–PLS-0). Washington, DC: U.S. Government Printing Office.

INTOSAI General Secretariat, International Standards of Supreme Audit Institutions. (2004). Guidelines for Internal Control Standards for the Public Sector—Further Information on Entity Risk Management I N T O S A I (INTOSAI GOV 9130). Vienna, Austria: INTOSAI General Secretariat—RECHNUNGSHOF (Austrian Court of Audit).

Kinnersley, R., and T. Patton. (2005). "GASB Statements 34 and 41." *The CPA Journal*. Retrieved from http:///www.nysscpa.org/cpajournal/2005/305/essentials/p20.htm.

Kirk, R. A. (2009). "Basic Accounting Techniques for Acquisition Librarians." In R. A. Kirk, *Basic Accounting Techniques for Acquisitions Librarians*. Charleston Conference, Charleston, SC.

Library of Congress. (2011). *Financial Statements: Fiscal 2010*. Retrieved from Library of Congress: http://www.loc.gov/about/reports/annualreports/.

Library of Congress. (2012). The Federal Library and Information Network. Retrieved from the Library of Congress, Federal Library and Information Network: http://www.loc.gov/flicc/fedlink/index_fedlink.html.

Michigan Department of Education. (2002). *Library of Michigan Financial Management Reference Guide*. Retrieved from http://www.michigan.gov/documents/hal_lm _finmanref1_66294_7.pdf.

Michigan State Budget Office, Department of Technology, Management and Budget. *Department of Technology, Management, & Budget, Glossary*. Retrieved from Michigan State Budget Office: http://www.michigan.gov/budget/0,1607,7-157-11460_11541- - -,00.html.

National Center for Education Statistics. (1998). *The Status of Federal Libraries and Information Centers in the United States: Results from the 1994 Federal Libraries and Information Centers Survey* (NCES 98-296). Washington, DC: U.S. Government Printing Office.

National Center for Education Statistics. (2002). *Public Libraries in the United States* (NCES 2002-308). Washington, DC: U.S. Government Printing Office.

National Center for Education Statistics. (2003). *Academic Libraries: 2000* (NCES 2004-317). Washington, DC: U.S. Government Printing Office.

National Center for Education Statistics. (2011). *Academic Libraries 2010: First Look* (NCES 2012-365). Washington, DC: U.S. Government Printing Office.

National Information Standards Organization. (2008). *SERU: A Shared Electronic Resource Understanding: A Recommended Practice of the National Information Standards Organization* [Standards NISO RP-7]. Retrieved from NISO.org: http://www.niso.org/publications/ rp/RP-7-2008.pdf.

National Information Standards Organization. (2012). *SERU Initiative Overview*. Retrieved from NISO.org: http://www.niso.org/workrooms/seru/seru_faq/.

OCLC. 2010. "How Libraries Stack Up." Retrieved from http://www.oclc.org/us/en/reports/ pdfs/214109usf_how_libraries_stack_up.pdf.

Office of Financial Management. (2001). *State Administrative & Accounting Manual* (80.20). Retrieved from the Office of Financial Management: http://www.ofm.wa.gov/policy/80 .20.htm.

Princeton Public Library Foundation. (2008). *Princeton Public Library Foundation, Investment Policy and Guidelines*. Retrieved from the Princeton Public Library Foundation: http:// foundation.princetonlibrary.org/files/StatementAmended11-10-08.pdf.

Raber, D. (2003). *The Problem of Information: An Introduction to Information Science*. Lanham, MD: Scarecrow Press.

Shepherd, P. T. (2005). COUNTER 2005: A New Code of Practice. *Learned Publishing* 18 (287–293).

Smith, G. R., Jr. Personal communication. 2009, 2012.

State Library of Iowa. *For Libraries—Telling the Library Story*. Retrieved from State Library of Iowa: http://www.statelibraryofiowa.org/ld/t-z/tell-library-story.

University of South Carolina. (2012). *Academic Bulletin*. Retrieved from University of South Carolina, Bulletin Search: http://bulletin.sc.edu/preview_program.php?catoid=35&poid=4209.

University of Wisconsin–Milwaukee. (2012). *Areas of Graduate Study*. Retrieved from University of Wisconsin Graduate School: http://www.graduateschool.uwm.edu/students/prospective/areas-of-study/.

U.S. Bureau of Labor Statistics. (2011). Occupational Outlook Handbook. In *Occupational Outlook Handbook, 2010–11 Edition*. Retrieved from http://www.bls.gov/oco/ocos023.htm.

Westchester Public Library. (2011). *Westchester Public Library Investment Policy*. Retrieved from Westchester Public Library: http://www.wpl.lib.in.us/policies/investment%20Policy.pdf.

Wisconsin Department of Public Instruction. (2008). *Administrative Essential: A Handbook for Wisconsin Public Library Directors Was Prepared by the Division for Libraries, Technology & Community Learning*. Retrieved December 13, 2011, from http://dpi.wi.gov/pld/ae13.html.

Index

About the Author

DR. RACHEL A. KIRK is an associate professor and collection management and acquisitions librarian at Middle Tennessee State University. She received her PhD in Communication and Information from the University of Tennessee, Knoxville in 2011, a master's degree in Information Sciences from the University of Tennessee, Knoxville, and a master's degree in Accounting from the University of North Carolina at Chapel Hill. She is a current member of the American Institute of Certified Public Accountants.